D0873756

Eight Steps to Raising Money

Measuring Your Fundraising Impact

For more information visit
www.thurgoodmarshallfund.org

© 2008 TMCF All Rights Reserved
All rights reserved under International and Pan-African Copyright Conventions. No part of this publication may be reproduced or transmitted in any form or by any means, electronic or mechanical, including photocopy, recording, or information storage and retrieval system, without the written permission of the author.

Published in the United States of America by Word for Word Publishing Co., Inc., Brooklyn, NY.

For book orders, author appearance inquiries and interviews, contact us by mail at:

Thurgood Marshall College Fund
RE: 8 Steps to Raising Money
80 Maiden Lane
Suite 2204
New York, NY 10038
Tel: (212) 573-8888
Fax: (212) 573-8497 or (212) 573-8554

or via the publisher at:

Word for Word Publishing Co., Inc.
Brooklyn, New York
718.222.WORD

The views expressed in this work are solely those of the author and do not necessarily reflect the views of the publisher, and the publisher hereby disclaims any responsibility for them.

ISBN-13: 978-1-8897325-3-4
ISBN-10: 1-889732-52-4

Printed in the United States of America

DEDICATION

This book is dedicated to the men and women who dedicated their lives to the profession of Fundraising and Development. Along the way, they have shaped my career through their commitment to nurturing the next generation of leaders for the profession.

Dr. N. Joyce Payne, Founder, Thurgood Marshall College Fund

Sylvia Brooks, Retired President, Houston Area Urban League, Inc.

Winfred Dunn, United Way, Texas Gulf Coast

Thomas W. Dortch, Jr., Former Chairman, 100 Black Men of America

The Late, James Cates, Area Director, United Negro College Fund

Johnny Parham, Jr., Retired Executive Director, Thurgood Marshall College Fund and Former, Area Vice President, United Negro College Fund

The Late, Ida Simon, Vice President Development, Lincoln University

Gene Templeton, Executive Director, Indiana University, School of Philanthropy

William H. Gray, Retired CEO, United Negro College Fund

Reginald Lewis, Former Executive Vice President, United Way, Essex County

Chris James Brown, Former President, United Way International

Dr. Lydia English, Program Officer, Andrew W. Mellon Foundation

Katy Ford, Former Vice President, Resource Development, United Way of the Texas Gulf Coast

Finally, this book is dedicated to all of my colleagues at the Thurgood Marshall College Fund, UNCF and United Way who have made philanthropy fun and fulfilling.

CONTENTS

"Being passionate about your cause is the key to fundraising success."

ACKNOWLEDGEMENTS

Over the years, I have received an abundance of calls soliciting fundraising advice and I have often wondered about a reader friendly book that would give people the basics of fundraising. However, in my opinion, a user friendly source for community volunteers to use does not exist. Hence, my reason for taking on this project. It took many years of countless mistakes, failures, sweat equity, hard work and ultimately, a lot of success to gain adequate knowledge to write this book. I would have been unable to preserver the task in front of me without the support of the people who mentored, challenged, advised, nurtured, tolerated my passion and coached me along the way. To all of you who have contributed to my growth and development and helped shape my career, I say thank you.

A very special thanks to my mother, Mary Gipson, who is on the Board of Directors of her church and is a community fundraiser—she always calls me for fundraising advice. Your questions helped to shape many of the chapters in this book. My friends who always serve as a source of support: Jim Clifton, Reginald Lewis, Brent Clinkscale, Debra Davis Ashley, Michael Fitzpatrick, Dwight Rhodes, Alicia Jackson, Sheila Kearney, Jennifer Jiles, Mark Melvin, Latoya Henry and Sharmagne Taylor.

The Thurgood Marshall College Fund staff who represent the best in class of non profit professionals. You guys always support me in everything I do. They are: Shineaca, Beverly, Lisa, Charisma, Shannon, Greg, Nicole, Susie, Deborah, Paul, Candice, Eve, Reggie, James, Atta, Christopher, Talesha, Melissa, Mykal, Patricia, Joy— Thank you for just being who you are individually. Larry Green, you are going to be an awesome executive fundraiser—I am proud of your growth.

To the awesome team of Fundraising Executives at the public HBCUs who have become my friends and colleagues. I am so proud to work with all of you.

Kenneth Austin, Tim Seiler, Joseph Suarez, and Dr. Lydia English, thank you for your friendship and endorsements of this project.

Finally, with great admiration and respect, Dr. N. Joyce Payne, founder of the Thurgood Marshall College Fund. Your "Social Entrepreneurship" serves as a model for others to emulate. I am so proud to have been able to work with you in advancing your legacy.

INTRODUCTION

Anyone can be called a fundraiser. However, few people can honestly say they are good at it. Some people have the passion necessary to support their cause, but lack planning and organizational skills. Others can create solid budgets but fail to motivate their volunteers. Many people have good intentions but are secretly scared to ask for money, which means their campaigns are doomed before they even get underway. Fortunately these problems can be overcome by following eight simple steps.

I am about to lead you through the fundraising process, from start to finish. By sticking to the eight steps outlined in this book, you will learn how to plan, execute, and complete a campaign that raises both money and your organization's standing in the community. Most importantly, I will teach you how to attract donors and then keep them involved so they contribute to your organization in the future.

I wrote this book primarily for two audiences. First, I considered the grassroots fundraiser. I'm talking about the dads who want to purchase new equipment for the Little League or the neighbors who decide they would like to improve their local park. These are people who want to support worthy projects but don't have a real grasp on how to bring their goals to fruition.

If you are new to raising money, the process can seem endlessly complicated and overwhelming. This book removes all of the uncertainty and gives you a solid recipe for success. Follow my guidelines and your fundraising campaign will be nearly failproof. I also wrote this book for entry-level professional fundraisers who need to obtain funds to achieve results for their organizations. If you fall into this category, you have even more at stake. Not only do you want to support your employer's initiatives, your personal career growth may depend on your fundraising ability. You won't be able to climb the ranks at work if you don't get results from your campaigns. Like many people in our field, you may have taken marketing or advertising courses in college. While those classes prepared you for some aspects of your job, most universities do not teach students how to effectively raise money. This book will help you become a savvy fundraiser, able to compete with other professionals fighting for the same limited donor dollars.

Think of fundraising as creating a great meal. It all starts with having the right ingredients. Why follow my particular recipe? It works. Every time. I have retooled and perfected this recipe during my 16 years as a professional fundraiser. I am currently chief executive officer and president of Thurgood Marshall College Fund (TMCF). Under my leadership, TMCF's revenues have increased by more than 700 percent. My team has raised $68 million by following the same basic strategies I will share with you in this book. Before joining TMCF, I achieved similar results for the United Way and the 100 Black Men of America, Inc., one of the nation's largest and oldest mentoring organizations. Using the same principals of fundraising, I spearheaded campaigns that increased 100 Black Men of America, Inc.'s annual revenues from $250,000 to $6 million. I also launched the organization's first capital campaign to raise $35 million.

While leading TMCF, colleagues have called my work "groundbreaking" and "unprecedented." I have received numerous awards, including an Honorary Doctorate of Laws from the University of the District of Columbia. While I'm humbled and flattered to be honored, I do not raise money to receive accolades. I raise money because I know I am serving an organization that makes a real difference in the lives of young people. Each dollar we receive means another African American will have a chance to join the ranks of the more than 5,000 Thurgood Marshall Scholars who have graduated and are making valuable contributions to our nation. While you may not have to raise the large amounts of money I do, our goals are essentially the same. Like me, you probably have great passion for your cause and a strong desire to change the lives of those you serve. With the right tools and strategies, you too can use fundraising to make a positive impact on the world.

Dwayne Ashley
Chief Executive Officer/President
Thurgood Marshall College Fund

CHAPTER 1

The First Step: Formulate Your Plan

Steps to Success

Anyone who has ever played sports knows that certain steps must be followed in order to excel on the field. You start with a good coach who understands the strategies behind the game, put players in positions based on their abilities, and stick to a regimen of practice and training. Sure, you could just stick a bunch of random guys on the field and hope for the best, but you'll never win many games. Why settle for losing when victory can be obtained with a bit of planning and effort? The same thing is true with fundraising. There are simple, easy-to-follow steps that will ensure your fundraiser is a success. Rushing ahead or skipping a step means risking failure. This book is going to give you the actions, listed in order, that will help you achieve your fundraising goals.

Why Hold a Fundraiser?

This question seems like a no-brainer. You want to raise money, right? Although raising money is your primary objective, there are other benefits to a well planned fundraising campaign.

Successful fundraisers:

- Generate positive publicity. A professional campaign will raise the community's awareness of and support for your project, making future donations to your organization more likely.
- Increase your army of volunteers. Your fundraising efforts not only attract donors, they help you increase the number of people who will give their time to your cause.
- Motivate your current members. Well-run campaigns give volunteers a common goal and sense of cohesiveness as a team. People like to be part of successful projects.

No one wants to continue to contribute time and effort to campaigns that don't succeed. Therefore, as you begin creating your organization's recipe for success, stay mindful of how actions during the planning stage will affect your future goals.

Passion is not Enough

Fundraising starts with passion. Your passion is the driving force behind your efforts to bring about positive change for your cause. However, passion and good intentions are not enough to create successful fundraisers. You need a defined plan of action. Let's say some parents want to raise money to purchase new equipment for their children's soccer team. At their first meeting, some of the parents immediately become very excited at the thought of planning an event fundraiser. One man raises his hand and suggests holding a car wash. A woman says, "That's a great idea! We can get the kids to help wash the vehicles." A third parent chimes in, "Maybe we could hold a bake sale at the same time. Customers can buy food while they wait for their car. My brother is a printer. I'll ask him to make some flyers!"

It is obvious that these parents are passionate and have good intentions, but this whirlwind approach will only set them up for failure because they have bypassed the crucial first step to raising money. They have not formulated their plan! Before you even think about what kind of fundraiser you want to have, you need to develop specific goals. This is true in every case, no matter how large or small the goals may seem. No exceptions.

Setting a Goal

Setting a goal is important because:
- You can't get someplace if you don't know where you are going. Without a set goal, no one will know if the fundraiser is a success.
- It is very difficult for volunteers to stay motivated and focused if they don't know exactly what they are trying to accomplish.
- Potential donors do not respond to only emotional pleas. They want to know how much money you want to raise and how their contributions will be utilized.

The Assessment

The first step in setting a realistic goal is to assess your needs. Do not rush this process. A full assessment will help you pinpoint your priorities and will be used to develop your budget.

Start your assessment by answering these questions:

- What do you want to operate?
- How many will the program serve?
- What will the real impact be on the people the program serves? Don't just say it will improve their lives. Be specific. For example, an after-school tutoring program will improve participants' test scores.
- How will you measure your impact? Will you monitor test scores of the children who are tutored? How will you chart their progress and when will you know that you have reached your goals?
- How long will the program be in effect? Will the after school program continue next year? If you are paying for improvements to a community park, will you raise money for a one-time purchase of park benches or will the improvements be staggered over time?
- What will be required to start the program? Be specific. In the example of the soccer team parents, just saying "soccer equipment" is not enough. Instead, the parents should make a list that might include 18 jerseys, 40 shin guards, 12 soccer balls, etc.
- What will be required to maintain the program?
- What types of emergencies or miscellaneous expenses might occur?

Once you know what your group needs are, find out how much each item on that list will cost. Your needs will determine your fundraising goals, not the other way around. Using the soccer parents as an example again, this would be the wrong approach to setting a goal:

"We should be able to raise $5,000," says the group leader.

"With the money, I think we can buy uniforms and equipment for our league. That may also leave enough left over to buy trophies for the winning team."

The leader has not given a compelling reason for trying to raise $5,000. In fact, he doesn't even seem sure that the amount will cover all items the league wants to purchase. If this group had taken time to conduct a full assessment of the program's needs, the leader would have been able to start the meeting by saying: "We have made a list priorities for this season. Our assessment shows that we will need $6,500 for next season. This will pay for equipment for only next year. Now, here is a breakdown of what this money will pay for…" Now that the parents know that they have to raise $6,500 for next season, they will use this figure to develop a fundraising budget. We'll discuss how to develop a budget later in this chapter.

How High to Set the Bar

In setting your financial goals for your campaign, you also have to be realistic about what your group is capable of raising. This can be tricky. You want to set the amount high enough that the people who care about your organization will challenge themselves to help you reach your goal. Many times at the end of a campaign, if volunteers and donors know that they are just a small amount away from reaching the target, they will push harder to come up with the required level of funding.

However, know the difference between a challenging goal and an unobtainable one. You should not set goals that you know will be very difficult to reach. Failing to hit a projected target can demoralize your team. If your volunteers and donors are not gratified by their experience and feel disappointed with themselves and the fundraiser, they may be not be around the next time you need them.

Do not make the opposite mistake of setting your fundraising goals too low. In tough times, it is easy to underestimate your donors. Don't sell your organization short. If you have a comprehensive plan of action and can make a solid case for that plan, you will get the help you need.

Identifying Your Stakeholders

Once you know how much money you are going to need, you have to figure out how you are going to get it. This will require an in-depth knowledge of your market, including the economic factors that shape the area. Form a small committee to help you with this. The committee members need to thoroughly understand the goals you are trying to reach. Most importantly, these should be people who understand what motivates your donors and how to persuade them to support your project.

Consider what you can realistically expect to get from your community. If you need one million dollars but you live in a town of only 8,000 people, then you better start broadening your support base. Ask yourself if your program benefits anyone on a larger regional level. Campaign everywhere you have impact, whether that be in your local town, county, state, or nationwide.

Mapping Your Stakeholders

Now, it is time to start thinking about the people in your campaign area who can contribute to your fundraiser. This process is called Mapping Your Stakeholders.

Stakeholders are people or groups that:

- Are members of your organization
- Either currently benefit from your program or have benefited from it in the past
- Have contributed to previous efforts
- Are sympathetic to the mission of your organization
- Have a connection to the program. For instance, if you are raising money for a youth sports team, contact the adults who played on the team when they were children.
- Could benefit from working with your organization. Think about the public relations potential of your project. Many companies might enjoy the positive publicity and increased name recognition they could receive from contributing to your fundraiser.

Don't forget to think about the existing members of your organization when you are setting your goals. These people are also key stakeholders. You need to be honest about their potential. Can they give more? How many of them will be able to contribute time and or money to this particular fundraiser? Do you have enough team members reach your goals? Brainstorm and think big. Compile a list of absolutely every organization or person who you think could be a stakeholder. Now that you have this list, it is time to come up with a Fund- raising Pyramid.

Creating a Fundraising Pyramid

Your fundraising pyramid will be used to develop a prospect list. A prospect list breaks down how much you think individual donors will be able to contribute. First, take a look at where your money came from in previous campaigns. Are these sources you can tap again? How much will you need to expand your donor base? To create your pyramid, start at the top. Let's say you need to raise $50,000. Is there someone who might be willing to give you that much? If so, what are you waiting for? Stop reading this book and pick up the phone. You might break the record for the world's fastest, successful campaign. Seriously, some fundraisers are able to achieve their goals with one well-placed phone call, but usually that is not the case. Next, figure out who might be able to give two gifts of $25,000. What five potential donors could make gifts of $10,000? What 20 prospects could give $2,500? Keep breaking this pyramid down until you reach a small, individual gift level. Once you create your prospect list, circulate it to your key stakeholders and committee members or discuss the list with them during one of your initial meetings. They may come up with people you haven't thought of. Your stakeholders will be your most effective tool in influencing the people they personally know to give money. Later, when you are ready for the next step, you will expand this pool of potential donors by meeting with your prospects face to face.

Identifying Competition and Naysayers

When planning a fundraiser, realize that you will almost always be facing competition. There have never been so many organizations fighting for the same donor dollars, and it is becoming increasingly difficult to stand out from the pack. According to the Internal Revenue Service, there are more than 800,000 charitable organizations in the United States. That's more than double the number that existed in 1990! More than half of these groups are small, perhaps like your organization, and rely on yearly revenues of less than $25,000. You have to consider who else is out there trying to raise money. Maybe your school group wants to sell giftwrap. That sounds like a good idea until you discover that three other groups in your school district are selling a similar product. It pays to research what campaigns other charities are running in your area. Avoid saturating your market with similar projects. However, just because someone else has used something, it doesn't mean you should stay away from the idea. You don't have to reinvent the wheel. If a fundraiser has worked for other charities in your area, consider the idea and then use it for inspiration to create your own unique project.

You will always be facing some sort of competition. Sometimes, you may also have to battle real opposition. It is a sad fact: not everyone is going to get on board with your plans. In fact, some people may actively oppose your goals. For instance, you may want to revive your neighborhood park, while a powerful developer in town would like to build condominiums on the land. These situations can rapidly become complicated. If you do not have the resources necessary to fight this kind of battle, you should consider joining forces with an existing group that shares your goals. If that group is larger and more organized, don't hesitate to abandon your own fundraising plans and concentrate your efforts on helping them succeed. One bigger, stronger organization will be able to achieve its goals easier than two smaller, weaker groups.

When facing opposition, look for support from some or all of the following:
- Chambers of commerce
- Religious groups
- Business leaders
- Labor groups
- Arts councils and organizations
- Philanthropists
- Community activists
- Social clubs
- Organizations promoting gender, race, or sexual orientation equality, such as the local branch of the NAACP or groups for women entrepreneurs.

Some of the people you contact will not want to get involved in your project, but just meeting with them will raise awareness of your issue, and you could build strong allies for future projects.

Choosing a Fundraiser

The fundraiser is the vehicle that will help you reach your financial goals. Picking a fundraiser is often the first thing a group does. This is a big mistake. Notice how this chapter is organized. As part of our recipe success, first you set your goals and then you identify your stakeholders. Only after you have done those two things are you ready to decide what kind of fundraiser would best serve your goals.

There are countless fundraising strategies. Some are closely associated with the groups that hold them. For instance, mention door-to-door cookie sales and people immediately think of the Girl Scouts. Politicians usually hold black-tie parties and dinners. School kids peddle gift wrap, cookie dough, and hoagie sandwiches. These are all proven fundraisers. Still, you should not rely on just one method of campaigning. The most successful fundraisers incorporate a variety of methods, including one-on-one meetings with potential donors, telemarketing, and special events.

When you and your fellow members are choosing a type of fundraiser, keep the following factors in mind:

- The scope of the fundraiser should match your goals: Do not pick a fundraiser that will not have the impact necessary to raise enough money. If you need to raise $25,000, you are not going to be able to reach that goal by holding one bake sale. On the other hand, don't pick a fundraiser that is too large for your goals. If you only need $1,000, there is no reason to throw a black-tie event.
- The size of your group: If your membership is small, it will be very difficult to hold an elaborate fundraiser. Conversely, not all fundraisers are geared toward large groups. You want something that everyone can take part in, but not something so big that members are overwhelmed.
- The strengths of your group: Know what your group is capable of handling. A group of senior citizens might be great at making telephone calls and face-to-face meetings. They may not have the physical stamina for fundraisers that require long periods of standing or strenuous activity.
- The strengths of individual members: Is there a member of your group who has a strong sales background? Does one

of your key stakeholders know a local celebrity who would agree to host a special event?

- The makeup of your membership: How old are your members and what are they primarily interested in? Most Boy Scouts are not going to want to sell flowers or scented candles, but they might enjoy holding a carwash. Your volunteers will naturally work harder on a project they enjoy.
- How the fundraiser can enhance your image in your community: Is this a fundraiser that will promote name recognition and give you some positive publicity?
- Does the fundraiser complement the mission of your organization: If you are a group that benefits children, you probably don't want to hold an Oktoberfest event featuring kegs of imported beer.
- What interests the people on your prospect list: Try to come up with something that will be fun for donors as well as volunteers. After all, these are the people who you rely on to keep the money rolling in. Don't make your donors dread coming to one of your events. Even the most diehard supporters don't want to sit through long speeches or have to eat bad food.

Establishing a Timeline

Many factors come into play when establishing a timeline for your fundraiser. First, consider when you will need the money you are raising. For instance, if you want to landscape a local park, you'll need to have the funding in place before the spring planting season begins. If you are raising money for an ongoing problem, like supporting breast cancer research, you will have more flexibility when building your timeline. Your timeline will also be determined by the scale of your campaign. Organizing a bake sale might not take more than a few weeks. Planning a black-tie charity auction with a celebrity host will take months.

Ideally, you want to have enough time to:
- Organize your volunteers.
- Make all necessary arrangements for the campaign, including details like buying supplies, hiring a band, printing t-shirts, etc.

- Get marketing materials in place.
- Let your prospects know about the campaign early enough that they can respond. When devising a timeline, you should work backwards, starting from the time your campaign needs to be finished. This will help you ensure that you start your fundraiser in enough time.

Here's how to pull your timeline together:
- List every task and detail that needs to be accomplished before the event.
- Beside each task, write how much time it requires. For example, your printer might need two weeks to create flyers.
- Next, mark your event day on a calendar.
- Make a list of everything that needs to be accomplished within 90 days of the event. Now list the tasks that need to be completed 60 days out, 30 days out, 2 weeks out, 1 week out, 2 days out, 1 day out, and the day of the event.
- Working backwards, fill in the dates on your calendar with the dates you should start and complete each task.

Make copies of your calendar for each member of your team or post a large calendar where everyone can see it. The entire staff should be aware of upcoming deadlines. Set realistic deadlines so your volunteers do not feel rushed. Also, make sure you leave a little flexibility for each deadline in case you have to deal with an unexpected problem, like a major snowstorm. If you are working with committees, designate a leader to enforce deadlines and monitor the progress of each committee's tasks. You do not want to miss a crucial benchmark because someone did not complete his or her job on time.

Figuring Out Your Budget

Unfortunately, before you can start raking in money, you are going to have to spend some. One of the keys to successful fundraising is to know how much it is going to cost you to reach your goals. At this point, your assessment has revealed how much money your organization wants to raise and you know which fundraising vehicle you are going to use. Now, it is time to add these two elements together. The amount of money your program will require to operate plus the costs of running your campaign add up to your fundraising budget.

The most important element in determining a budget is that you identify everything that will cost you money. You do not want to be surprised by hidden expenses. The items included on a budget vary from fundraiser to fundraiser. *Some common expenses include:*

- Renting a site (if you are holding a special event)
- Food and drinks
- Marketing costs, including printing, advertising, and postage
- Equipment rental, such as tables and chairs, microphones,
- Entertainment costs, such as hiring a band
- Inventory that will be sold to raise money
- Telephone expenses
- Prizes or giveaways
- Transportation
- Miscellaneous items, including pens, notepads, etc.

You will now need to build these costs into your goal. So, if the soccer parents want to clear $6,500 and they estimate that it is going to cost $1,000 to hold their fundraiser, then their total campaign goal needs to be $7,500. Expect your campaign expenses to comprise 10 to 40 percent of your total budget. Although it is common for 50 percent of the money raised by organizations to go to campaign-related costs, this is not a responsible use of your donors' money. You should try to reduce that percentage as much as possible. One of the best ways to save money is to get one of your major campaign items donated. For example, if you are holding an auction, find out if your stakeholders know someone who would be willing to provide the site or necessary equipment for free.

Another way to offset expenses is to find a sponsor. Unlike a stakeholder, sponsors get something in return for their contribution, usually in the form of publicity. For example, if you are holding a walk-a-thon, you might offer to put the name of your sponsor on your signs and posters. Sometimes sponsors will even provide their own signage or giveaway items, which reduces your costs even further. For example, a local bank might give you money for the seed costs at the beginning of the walk-a-thon and then later provide water cups printed with the bank's logo that you can give to the walkers.

Just remember, that sponsors are donors, not event organizers. Beware of sponsors that try to exert control over your fundraiser. Even the most well-planned campaigns will encounter unexpected costs, so it is a good idea to keep your budget flexible. You will often have to update your budget while the campaign is underway. Just don't let costs skyrocket! Remember, your ultimate goal is not to sell cookies or hold a golf tournament.

Fundraisers are only a tool to get money, not to spend it. Keep a close eye on spending and use restraint at all times. Your stakeholders will appreciate smaller, simpler fundraisers. They don't want their money spent on fancy meals or expensive advertising campaigns. Next, go through the following checklist to make sure you have not skipped any of the components of formulating your plan. Once your plan is complete, you are ready for Step 2: Making Your Case.

Formulate Your Plan
The Checklist
> Complete Your Assessment. Be specific.
- Who you are going to serve?
- Exactly how many will benefit?
- How will they benefit?
- How will you measure the program's impact?
- How long will the program continue?
- What will you need to accomplish your goals?
- What will be the cost of each item you need?

> Map Your Stakeholders
- Know what your community can afford to give.
- List your stakeholders.
- Create a fundraising pyramid.
- Fill-in prospects on the pyramid.
- Circulate the prospect list to your stakeholders.
- Ask stakeholders to expand the prospect list.

> Identify Your Competition
- Learn about groups similar to yours in your area.
- Find out if they are holding fundraising campaigns.

- Examine how their campaigns are similar and different from yours.
Identify Naysayers
  - Find out if someone is likely to work against your efforts.
  - Develop a plan to overcome naysayers.
  - Consider joining forces with other groups that share your goals.

> Choose a Fundraiser
  - Does it fall between 10 to 40 percent?
  - Does the size of the fundraiser match your goals?
  - Is it something that your group can handle?
  - Does it utilize the strengths of your members, both as individuals and as a group?
  - Will the fundraiser also raise positive public awareness of your organization?

> Establish a Timeline
  - Know when you have to have the campaign completed.
  - List all required tasks.
  - Work backwards from the campaign completion date, listing the order in which all tasks must be started and finished.

Measuring Your Fundraising Impact
Create a Budget
  - List all your fundraising expenses.
  - Add your fundraising expenses together to reach a total.
  - Add fundraising total expenses to your initial goal (developed in the assessment).
  - Compute the percentage of your campaign that will have to go to fundraising expenses. Note this percentage. Does it fall between 10 to 40 percent
  - List creative ways that you can reduce campaign expenditures.

You've figured out what type of campaign you are going to run; now you need to sell it. But before you can begin to approach donors and sponsors or think about marketing your project, you need a game plan. Too often, inexperienced fundraisers just assume that if they are working for a good cause, donors will appreciate their efforts and automatically contribute money. They expect their campaign to sell itself. Don't make this mistake. You need to build a case that tells your donors why your program is worthwhile and why they should support you now. Knowing how to make a case is the difference between fundraisers who make a lot of money and those who don't. More nonprofit organizations and charities are trying to raise money than ever before. Your donors get many requests from other worthy organizations just like yours. At the same time, the public's trust of charities has eroded, thanks to a few high profile cases involving the misuse of donated money. Donors are less likely to give as blindly as they have in the past. They want to know exactly how their contributions are going to be spent and who will be benefiting from the program.

CHAPTER 2

The Second Step: Make Your Case

Why Your Campaign?

Quick, answer this question: Why is your campaign important?
Did you immediately think of a succinct, one- or two- sentence answer, or did you find yourself saying, "Umm.. well, we'd really like to help kids because.. umm..."? It is crucial that you can clearly articulate why your efforts matter. If you don't know why your project is important, then no one else ever will. It is a good idea to come up with one or two sentences that summarize why donors should care about your campaign. Think about what makes your project unique. For example, let's say you want to raise money for your local animal shelter. That's nice, but not unusual. A lot of people raise money to help animal shelters. Dig a little deeper. Perhaps your shelter is the only one in town that has a foster care program. Your statement could be, "ABC Shelter is the only shelter in Anytown that finds loving foster homes for dogs and cats. We are raising money to pay for vaccinations the animals need before they can go to their new homes."

Quantify Your Impact

Now that you can articulate why your program is valuable, take it one step further and quantify your impact. Quantifying your impact means measuring the outcome of your project. Do not underestimate the importance of this step. Quantifying the impact of your program is the single most important way you show that you are accountable to your donors. When you quantify the impact of your campaign, donors see that their contributions are being put to good use. You are giving them a tangible way to see why your mission is effective.Quantify your goals by answering the following questions:

- Who will you serve?
- How many people will be served?

- What problem are you trying to address with your program?
- What kind of impact will your program have on them?
- What change will it bring about in their lives?
- How many of those served will actually experience the benefit of the impact? For example, out of 125 senior citizens taking part in your program, at least 25 percent will be able to reach and maintain their fitness goals over the course of one year.
- How will you measure the change?

Remember, quantifying your impact means giving exact numbers and specific outcomes. In the case of the animal shelter, you could quantify the impact by building on your previous statement. Now you could say, "ABC Shelter is the only shelter in Anytown that finds loving foster homes for dogs and cats. We are raising $2,000 to pay for the vaccinations 200 animals will need before they can go to their new homes." To illustrate this point further, let's say we want to start an after-school program at our local community center. Here's how we would quantify our impact:

- Who? The program targets kids between the ages of 8 and 18 who use the park where the community center is located.
- Number of kids? There are 1,000 kids currently using the park and community center. We hope to enroll 250 in the new program.
- Current problem? There is nothing in the neighborhood that offers something constructive for the kids to do after school. Additionally, the school dropout and failure rates are high because children are getting involved with drugs and/or gang activity.
- Impact? We will benefit children by giving them a safe place to spend time after school and providing them with tutoring and help with homework.
- Number affected? We believe we can increase graduation rates for the children involved in our program by 10 percent, while improving overall test scores.
- Measure? Over a five-year period, we will measure the percentage of kids in our program who graduate from high

school against the percentage of teenagers from the same neighborhood who are not enrolled in the after-school program. We will also track each child's report cards and provide tutoring in subjects where they need extra help.

The Multiplier Effect

When quantifying your impact, don't forget the multiplier effect. This is the impact your program will have on people who are beyond the scope of your concentrated efforts. For example, Thurgood Marshall College Fund (TMCF) creates a college guide that we send to 17,000 school districts. Our direct beneficiaries are the 35,000 faculty and students who initially receive a copy. However, we know that our direct beneficiaries often give the guide to other students and their families after they have read it. These other students and families are the indirect beneficiaries. We estimate that more than 125,000 indirect beneficiaries use our material. Therefore, we include these beneficiaries when we quantify the impact of our college guides.

Although you want to include your direct and indirect beneficiaries when you quantify your impact, don't try to inflate the number of people you serve just so you can have impressive numbers. Be realistic about your goals. Big is not always better. In fact, sometimes smaller programs can have a much larger benefit to the individuals they serve. For instance, if you are working with a $50,000 budget, you could try to serve 5,000 people. However, if you focus your efforts on serving 500 people, you will have the resources to make a much larger impact on their lives.

CREATE A PRESENTATION PACKET

Now that you can articulate the importance of your project and know how to quantify your goals, it is time to create a professional, written plan. This is called a presentation packet. You will take your presentation packet with you when you visit your donors. It does not have to be fancy or elaborate. A simple folder containing a few sheets of paper highlighting your campaign is fine. In fact, people who give to small fundraisers will probably be suspicious of how you utilize contributions if it looks like you spent a lot of money on printing materials.

Your presentation packet should:
- Succinctly explain the need for your project – the shorter the better. Don't bore your donors with minute details, but do explain why your campaign is important.
- Quantify your impact. As I've already explained, you need to be very clear about the benefits your project will have on those you serve.
- Briefly explain your budget. Donors want to know how you are going to spend their donations. Give a breakdown of your major expenditures. If they know exactly how the money is going to be used, they may be inclined to give more money to help you meet your goals.

Other items in your presentation packet should include:
- Your contact information. Make it easy for your donors to reach you.
- Information on your organization. Explain how long you've been in existence, why and how your group was formed, and who is on your board or steering committee.
- A pledge envelope
- Buttons, pins, bumper stickers, or other promotional materials. These are nice to include, but not necessary if you do not already have these items or are working on a small budget.
- Depending on your campaign, you can also provide a description of gift-giving levels and what can be achieved by giving at each level. For instance, "A $25 dollar gift pays for one child's uniform..."

When writing your presentation packet, don't use clichés or overly flowery speech. Instead, keep your language simple and upbeat. The goal is to use words that express the passion and excitement you feel for your project, without going overboard and sounding hackneyed. Instead of using a lot of copy, list your key ideas in bullet points. In presentation packets, a few quick nuggets of information will have more impact than several paragraphs of detailed explanation. Although it is a good idea to get input from your team members, make sure only one person writes the presentation packet in order to keep the "voice" consistent. Again, don't worry about making your packet elaborate. Just keep it simple and neatly organized so it is easy for your donors to pick it up and get your message quickly.

The Checklist

> *Why you?*
>
> - One or two sentences about what makes your program important and unique
>
> *Quantify your impact by answering the following questions:*
> - What problem do you want to solve with your program?
> - Who will you serve?
> - What is the total number of people you will serve?
> - What percentage of those served will be positively changed by the experience?
> - How will you measure your success?
>
> *Create a presentation packet*
> Make sure you include:
> - "Why You" statement
> - How you quantify your impact
> - Budget information
> - Information on your organization, including its history, mission, and leaders
> - Contact information
>
> *Optional items:*
> - Pledge envelope
> - Bumper stickers, pens, or other small giveaway items
> - Description of gift-giving levels

To pull off your campaign, you're going to need a motivated and energetic team. This team should consist of a leader, a leadership team or board, and your army of volunteers. Right now, you might not have any trouble rounding up troops. Everyone loves working on a fundraising campaign—in the beginning! The key is keeping them passionate until the project wraps up. It all starts with the leader.

"Plan, plan, plan and then plan more is the key to success."

CHAPTER 3

The Third Step: Build Your Team

Picking a Leader

Choosing a leader is the first big decision when running a campaign. In fact, it is THE decision. Without leadership, even the most inspired ideas will never go anywhere. Are you the leader? If you immediately answered "yes," are you sure? You might have picked up this book or come up with the campaign idea, but that doesn't mean that you will be the best leader for this project. Maybe you are the most qualified leader available, but maybe you're not. If you want your fundraising efforts to succeed, you have to put your ego aside and make decisions that are best for the campaign.

You can't lead if no one wants to follow you. A good leader is someone who:
- Understands the mission. Leaders know the details — all of them.
- Communicates goals. Communication is essential to the functioning of the team. A good leader makes sure everyone understands his or her individual job and how it fits within the project.
- Stays organized. This is a job that requires juggling paperwork, phone calls, and staff issues, all at the same time and all under a deadline.
- Serves as a cheerleader -Not only do leaders have to stay motivated, they have to keep everyone else pumped up. Do not underestimate the difficulty of this task.
- Makes decisions. This is not a job for the wishy-washy.
- Is flexible. The best leaders don't just rigidly bark out orders. They are constantly listening and adapting. They are sensitive to those around them and act accordingly.

- Delegates. Leaders know when to ask for help. Once they assign jobs, they are able to let others do their work without micromanaging.
- Stays calm. Leaders are most effective when they can stay unruffled and focused in stressful situations.

Your Leadership Team

Your leadership team or board will help organize your efforts from start to finish. Typically, each leadership team member will focus on a specific aspect of your project, such as marketing or overseeing volunteers. Large fundraising organizations have very structured boards, often using CEOs from major companies to boost their pubic profile. Because this book is for grassroots fundraisers and small campaigns, I am not going to discuss the ins and outs of creating this type of structured board. Instead, I will focus on leadership teams that are small and hands-on.

When selecting members of your leadership team, choose individuals who:

- Clearly understand the mission. Everyone must be on the same page.
- Have adequate time to contribute. Good ideas are not enough. Fundraising takes a lot of time and effort.
- Have connections within the community. Your leadership team members should have a network of contacts that can provide donations and sponsorships.

Leadership Meetings

Even if your leadership team is made up of three best friends, don't make the mistake of being too casual. Your meetings should have some type of structure.

The leader should start each meeting with a clear agenda that is shared with members of the team. Someone should be in charge of recording minutes, which basically means writing down the key decisions and plans that you discuss. Keep your meetings restricted to members of the leadership team. Letting extra people attend usually just leads to extra voices and extra distractions. Also, keep your eye on the time. Your meetings should have a scheduled start and end time. Save socializing for before and/or after the meeting.

Engaging the Troops

Usually, you will find volunteers from within your organization. After all, these are the people who care most about your program. However, you can also get new volunteers through hanging flyers, posting on Internet forums, and word of mouth. You know why you need volunteers, but what do they get out of the deal? Most volunteers sign up because they fit into one of these categories:

- They or someone they know directly benefits from your programs.
- They believe in your cause and have a strong desire to help your organization.
- They want to meet new people while doing something fun and constructive.
- They want to advance their career, either by networking within your organization or by learning professional skills, such as building a computer database.

You will get the most out of your volunteers if you understand why they want to be involved in your campaign. Give them a job they enjoy and they will work harder and stick with it longer. When meeting new volunteers, ask a lot of questions. Listen to their goals and try to assess their skill level. Start them off with smaller tasks, so you can get a feel for their ability without overwhelming them. Explain that they will be able to take on more responsibility (if they want it) as they become more familiar with the organization.

Volunteer Meetings

Your volunteers will be most engaged in the process when they have a clear understanding of what is expected of them. Have a group meeting to brief your volunteers on the campaign, your goals, and the exact jobs they will perform. Be specific about their duties. A list of topics for the first volunteer meeting should include:

- An overview of the program. Your volunteers should already know about your organization, but getting a refresher course or learning a few new details is always helpful.
- Why you are holding this campaign. Discuss what problems you hope to solve or programs you want to implement by raising money now.
- How you plan to raise the money. These are the specifics of the campaign.
- The goals of the campaign
- The job of the leadership team
- What is expected of volunteers
- Who volunteers can contact if they have a problem
- What decisions volunteers can make and what decisions must be made by the leadership team.

Ask for a Pledge

Volunteers always have good intentions. Unfortunately, they can also have very short attention spans. Unlike major fundraising operations, you probably will not have a set of bylaws or board members to keep everyone in check. Therefore, you have to rely on promises. I recommend that you ask everyone to make a pledge to do the job they are assigned. This includes each volunteer and member of your leadership team. Explain to them that their work is important. You will need their attention from the time they sign up until the campaign is finished. If they can not commit to the entire process, you would prefer they help the organization in another way.

Volunteers = Donors

I also require that my volunteers and leaders be donors. They do not have to give a lot of money, but they must give something. Making a donation gives them ownership of the campaign. They are more likely to feel a responsibility to a project they have contributed to. Making donations also gives them more credibility when approaching prospects. When my volunteers talk to donors, I want them to be able to say, "I have given my gift of $XX, can I ask you to do the same?"

Taking Care of Your Troops

Remember to take care of your volunteers. They are not working for a paycheck. They are working for intangible benefits that may be fleeting. Since you are relying on their passion, you can keep their motivation high by always remembering to:

- Say "thank you!" There are all kinds of volunteer recognition programs. You can give out awards, make announcements, or have dinners. However, I find that the single best way you can motivate volunteers is by personally thanking them. When you see your volunteers doing a good job, stop for a moment and acknowledge their work. No one likes to feel unappreciated. Let them know you value their efforts.

- Feed them. When your volunteers are working, provide refreshments. It's a way of keeping them comfortable and showing your appreciation for their work. A plate of cookies, pots of coffee, and beverages can go a long way toward boosting morale.

- Don't overwhelm them. Give volunteers jobs that they can easily handle. New volunteers should always be given simple jobs. As soon as they start to feel stressed, the work will no longer feel rewarding. It won't take long before they stop showing up.

Build Your Team
The Checklist

Your leader should be:

- Clear on the mission
- Able to communicate goals
- Organized
- A cheerleader
- A decision maker
- Flexible
- Able to delegate
- Able to stay calm
  > Your Leadership Team should
  - Understand the mission
  - Have the time available for the campaign

- Have a supply of networking contacts in the community

Your volunteers need to know:

- The mission of your organization
- Why you are holding this campaign
- How you will run the campaign
- The financial goals
- The job of the leadership team
- The job each volunteer will do
- What is expected of all volunteers
- Who they can contact if they have a problem
- What decisions they can make
- What decisions must be made by the leadership team

All volunteers and leadership team members should:

- Make a pledge or promise of support
- Make a financial donation
  > Take care of your volunteers
  - Say "thank you!"
  - Feed them
  - Don't overwhelm them

CHAPTER 4

The Fourth Step: Meet Your Donor

Ask, Ask, Ask

This may be the most important thing you will read in this book: If you want money, you have to ask for it. You may think this sounds like a no-brainer, but let me explain. Many fundraisers (maybe even you) are afraid to ask. They can dream up creative campaigns, plan well and motivate volunteers, but when it comes time to actually ask for money, knots form in their stomach.

Occasionally, a person will hear about your organization or campaign and decide to send you some money unsolicited. That can, and hopefully will, happen – but it will not happen very often. So, since money usually won't come to you, you will have to go after it. And that means asking. In fundraising, there are many variables. However, there is one thing you can count on: People will not give unless they are asked. When you ask them, many will still not give. Therefore, you will have to do a lot of asking to reach your goals.

Conquering Fears

If you are afraid to ask for money, you will need to deal with your anxiety before you can become an effective fundraiser. The fear you feel is understandable, but it is not natural. You were not born afraid of asking for money. You learned it. Your parents probably taught you that when visiting friends or relatives you should be polite, wait until someone offers you something instead of asking for it, and not to talk about money. To learn how to fundraise effectively, you are going to have to set aside two of those three rules. (You still have to be polite!) In many other cultures, talking about money is commonplace. It is not considered rude to ask how much someone earns or what they paid for their home. However, in the United States, we believe money is "private" and not to be discussed. This discretion may still be appropriate in some areas of your life, but it is counterproductive to fundraising. Ask yourself what is more important to you, obtaining money for your organization or holding onto learned fears?

Why Ask for a Meeting?

The best way to ask for money is to do it face to face. People give to other people, not organizations. To illustrate this point, I want you to pretend that you are your potential donor. You pick up your mail and find a letter asking you to support a worthy cause. If you are like most people, you read the top line and then set it aside to see what else is in your stack of mail. Even if you read the entire letter and find yourself moved and willing to donate, will you immediately get your checkbook, write out a check and mail it? Of course not. You'll place it somewhere with a mental promise to "get to it later." Later may never come.

Now, pretend you are a sitting face to face with the person who wrote the letter. Instead of reading words on a page, you hear the passion and commitment in their voice as they explain how you can make a difference. You are now far more likely to respond by picking up your checkbook.

The first rule of going to a meeting is that you have to be prepared, very prepared. You need to know exactly why your donor should help fund your campaign. Rereading the presentation packet you created will be helpful, but you should learn how to take those words off of the page and breathe life into them. This is your "story" and it is crucial that you know how to tell it. Your story should not be longwinded. A good story is a condensed version of what makes your organization worth supporting.

Your story should include the organization's:

- History. How long it has operated, who started it, and why
- Benefits. How it helps those it serves, including at least one short uplifting anecdote to illustrate the point. This can come from your beneficiary, which I'll explain in the next section.
- Quantified Impact. How you measure your impact. Again, this is very specific. For example, 'Out of the 200 children

we've tutored, more than 80 percent have gone up at least one letter grade in reading."

You will tell this story each time you meet a potential donor. It is important that you believe your story. You should feel enthusiastic and passionate about sharing it. If you are only acting out your story, not speaking from the heart, people will be able to tell that you are not genuine. Not only will they be less likely to give, they'll probably feel uncomfortable or insulted and want nothing to do with you in the future. Even when you tell a good story, people will frequently tell you "no." Think about possible objections you may face and be prepared to offer a gently persuasive response for each. If you are new to conducting meetings, get members of your team to help you through role playing. They can pretend to be your donor. Give them your best pitch and then let them try to stump you with tough questions, wishy-washy offers of support, and outright refusals.

Setting Up Meetings

If you have completed step one, you should have no trouble setting up meetings with potential donors. Use your list of stakeholders, starting with the people and organizations at the top of your fundraising pyramid. Have your team members make the initial calls to potential donors they personally know. By calling stakeholders, you dramatically increase your chances of obtaining a face-to-face meeting. Unlike cold calling, they already know about your organization and their philanthropic interests match your mission. When setting up a meeting, try to go to your donor's home or business. Do not expect or invite them to come to you for the first meeting. There are three primary reasons for this:

- You'll have a better chance of getting a meeting if they do not have the inconvenience of travel.
- It can appear impolite to assume they should have to come to you.
- The initial meeting is held to find out more about them, their needs, and their interests. Therefore, it should be on their turf.

After the first meeting, you can offer to give them a tour of your organization or take them to see your beneficiaries. Occasionally, donors will express interest in visiting you first. If that is the case, honor their request, but still keep most of the meeting focused on them and save extended tours for a later visit. If donors cannot fit you into their schedule, ask if they would be available for a brief telephone meeting. This will show that you respect their time, but still believe they are an important part of your efforts.

Who Goes with You

Now that you have the meeting, it is time to decide who should go with you. Be very selective and keep the number small. Never bring someone to a meeting unless you are certain he or she will make a valuable contribution to the discussion. If too many people go, you run the risk of making your donor feel outnumbered and overwhelmed. I suggest a team of three people: you (assuming you are the campaign leader), a member of the board or someone on your leadership team, and a beneficiary. Each one will play an important role. The leader represents the organization. It is the leader's job to explain your mission and campaign. If I don't personally know the donor, I like taking a board member who does. Even if they haven't met each other, board members are a valuable part of the meeting because they represent fellow donors. After all, they make monetary contributions too (or at least they should!).

When meeting with donors, my board members do not hesitate to make statements such as, "I financially support TMCF by giving a gift in the range of $XX a year. Is this a level of support that you think you can match?" I also almost always take a beneficiary with me to meetings. Beneficiaries can speak first hand about the impact your program has. They provide a "face" for your campaign. Give them a few minutes to tell their story. In my case, TMCF beneficiaries are college students who receive our scholarships. Although I can tell donors about how TMCF allows deserving students get an education, it is far more effective for donors to listen to actual students explain how their lives have changed because of support from donors, just like them.

The Presentation

Start your presentation by letting your donor know what you are going to cover. You might say, "Today we are going to talk about our mission, why we exist, and what we plan to accomplish with our current campaign. We also want to know what you think of our goals, get any of your suggestions, and hopefully get you more involved in our project."

Making Connections

Now, it's time to get started. You want your entire presentation to last less than 15 minutes. It helps to create an outline of main points you wish to make. However, use the outline mostly to mentally prepare for the meeting. During the meeting, you can glance at the outline, but do not read from it or other prepared notes. You want to establish a personal connection with your donor. Connections can only be made if you are able to maintain eye contact and friendly conversation. Try to always present your case in a way that feels like a discussion, not a lecture. You'll know you are on track if your donor feels free to interject questions and comments during your presentation.

When giving your presentation:
- Keep each point brief. Do not get sidetracked or take too long exploring any one idea.
- Show enthusiasm. You donor needs to feel your passion in order to be excited about your campaign. Express why this is a project worth supporting.
- Don't lean on crutches. Some people rely heavily on visual aids such as PowerPoint presentations. They might be effective, but they can never replace eye contact. If you want to use a visual aid to make a point, do so, and then immediately go back to your conversation. Don't make your donor sit through a scripted slideshow.
- Ask questions. If your donor is not asking questions, then you should. Something as simple as, "What do you think is the value of this program?" will help keep the conversation flowing.
- End on an uplifting note. Explain plans for future growth. Describe how you think your program can have a long-term impact with continued support from donors like them.

Here is a general outline that you can use to structure your presentation.

> Intro
   • What You Will Cover
> Organization's Mission
   • Who you serve (your beneficiaries)
   • The needs or problems you address
   • The impact on your beneficiaries
> Current Campaign
   • The goals of your current campaign
   • How the campaign serves your overall mission
   • How you will quantify your impact
   • Brief explanation of the program's budget
> Looking to the Future
   • Plans for growth
   • Long-term impact on beneficiaries
> Engage the Donor (possible questions)
   • Did anything I've talked about surprise you?
   • What do you like about the current campaign? Or dislike?
   • Do you have any suggestions for strengthening either the current campaign or organization as a whole?

Making the Ask!

Before you go to the meeting, decide who is going to make "the ask," which is the direct request for financial support from your donor. Never choose the beneficiary. It is tacky and will look unprofessional. That leaves you and your board member or individual from your leadership team. Choose which one of you will make the ask based on the following:

   • Who is most comfortable asking for money? This is the most important factor. If you look uncomfortable, your donor will be uncomfortable. Asking for a contribution should feel like a natural part of a flowing discussion. It should never create an awkward situation.
   • Who has the best track record? Asking for money is a skill developed through experience. The person who has the most finesse is often the best choice.
   • Who knows the donor the best? A personal relationship will further smooth the asking process.

Once you know who is going to make the ask, you need to know when to make it. Generally, the ask comes toward the end of the meeting, after you have answered all of the donor's questions about your campaign. However, there are no hard rules about timing. I usually feel like it is a bit of a dance between the two parties. I know the direction the meeting is headed, but I don't want to make the move too soon. I watch donors for signs that they are ready to discuss making a gift and then make the ask. When making the ask, never request a specific dollar amount. Instead, suggest a range of giving. Do not say, "We are asking you today for $25,000." Say, "We would like you to consider making a pledge of support in the range of $25,000," or "We're looking for leaders to support us at the $25,000 level." The difference is subtle, but significant. By suggesting a range of support or a gift level, you let the donor know what you would like, but still allow them control over the exact amount.

The Close

The final moments of the meeting is called "the close." Use this time wisely because it sets the stage for the next phase in the relationship with your donor. During your close, thank the donor for taking the time to meet with you. Also ask the following questions:

- Do you have any more questions about our organization?
- Is there anything else I can do for you or get you?
- When can I follow up?

That last question is very important. Don't just say, "I'll call you in three days." Let donors tell you when you can make the next contact. Then honor their wishes. If they tell you to call in two weeks, don't call next week. Always end the meeting with both of you knowing what the next step will be and when it will happen.

Thank You

Within 24 hours of the meeting, send a handwritten note to donors thanking them for meeting with you and to let them know you will be contacting them at the agreed-upon time. It is also a good idea to mention something interesting you discussed. Then, let them know that you are looking forward to their support. Above all else, keep it brief. This is a thank-you note, not another presentation.

Here is an example of a thank-you note:

Dear Ms. Smith,

Thank you for taking the time to speak with me yesterday. I enjoyed our discussion immensely. You had some great ideas about spreading our message. Based on your suggestion, I am going to contact Mr. Brown about donating printing materials.

I'll give you a call next Tuesday to talk more about supporting ABC Soccer League. Thanks to generous supporters like you, we'll give 250 underprivileged children a new field to play on this year!

Sincerely,
Melinda Holtz

Face-to-Face Basics

When conducting a personal appeal, you'll have much greater success if you adhere to the following rules:

- Arrive on time. Being late is not only unprofessional, it shows a lack of respect for your donor's time.
- Stick to time limits. If your donor says he or she can only give you 30 minutes, do not stick around for 45.
- Be brief. Your donors hear these types of presentations all the time. As soon as they start to look at the clock, you've lost them.
- Create a personal connection. Show that you value them by remembering the names of their children, asking about their hobbies, or congratulating them on recent accomplishments. Just don't babble. This is a business meeting. And remember, not everyone likes small talk, so never force conversation.
- Don't do all of the talking. We've covered this, but it is so important, I want to stress it again. Ask them about their thoughts on your organization's mission, efforts, and campaign. Your stakeholders will often have great ideas, not

to mention contact with other potential donors. Allowing them to share their ideas will not only give you new insight, it will show them that you value them for more than just their money. Your contributors do not want to feel like they are regarded only as ATMs.

- Be persistent, but don't pressure. It is important that you are persuasive in your presentation, but learn to take "no" for an answer. No one owes you a contribution. In fact, they don't even owe you a good reason for not giving money. If they say "no" now, they may eventually change their mind when you politely follow up after the meeting. Hard-sell techniques will only alienate your stakeholders from donating in the future.

- Know what you want. You would not ask a wealthy donor for a $25 contribution, just like you wouldn't ask a struggling family for a $25,000 gift. You should have established the amounts you will ask for when creating your Fundraising Pyramid. To get what you want, you need to ask for a level of support, and that level or range must be appropriate for the donor.

- Follow up. After your meeting, follow up with the handwritten letter we've discussed. Then continue to keep donors informed on your organization's progress and how their contributions are being utilized.

Final Thoughts on Meetings

I'd like to give you one last piece of advice before you head off to your first meeting. Remember that your donors give you more than money. They give you their trust when they write a check. They will never make contributions if they do not have faith in your mission or your ability to bring your goals to fruition. You earn trust over time by showing that you are a good steward of their contributions. Also, do not go into a meeting focused only on making your Sales pitch. Sure, a hard sell may get you one check, but they'll probably never want to meet with you again. Respect your donor. Show that you care about what is important to them and you'll have an important relationship in years to come.

Meet Your Donor
The Checklist
Preparing for a Meeting
- Know your story.
- Practice telling your story and answering questions.

> Who To Take
- Campaign organizer
- Board member or member of leadership team
- Beneficiary

The Presentation Outline
- Intro: Explain what you will discuss.
- Mission: Who you serve, needs addressed, and impact on beneficiaries
- Current campaign: goals, how the campaign fits with overall mission, how you will quantify its impact, and budget
- Future plans: Growth and long-term impact
- Questions to donor: suggestions, likes, and dislikes

> Making the Ask
- Decide who will make the ask.
- Know what range or level of gift you will ask for.

The Close
- Answer any additional questions.
- Discuss the next steps, including when you can contact the donor.

Thank-You Note
- Make it handwritten.
- Send within 24 hours of meeting.

Motivational letters are a vital part of your campaign. A carefully crafted letter can motivate your donors and inspire them to enthusiastically support your campaign. A carelessly written letter will just end up in the trash.

CHAPTER 5

The Fifth Step: Write a Motivational Letter

Who and When

A personal letter will remind your donors that you are still out there and that you value their contributions and input. Most importantly, it will give you another chance to reinforce your campaign's message. You should send letters only to people you have already had contact with. Most people unfamiliar with your organization will just consider an unsolicited letter they receive as junk mail. Trying to create an emotional connection with strangers can be done, but that falls into the realm of direct mail, which is usually a job best left to large organizations. Grassroots fundraisers will find that sending "cold" letters is a waste of time and postage. Instead of mailing letters to people who don't know your organization, focus on sending motivational letters to:

- Welcome new donors. Greet new members and let them know that you are thrilled to have them onboard. This establishes a personal connection, encourages them to offer financial support now and lays the groundwork for future, and hopefully larger, gifts in the future.
- Reach stakeholders. These people already know and support you. A letter can strengthen your connection to them and keep them informed about how they can help you in your latest efforts.

The Message

When writing your letter, you should convey your message in a way that is sincere, direct, and succinct. You want them to know why this campaign is important and how they can help reach its goals. Keep the message short. You do not need to include extraneous details.

Make sure your message includes answers to each of these questions:

- What is your shared affinity? In other words, what do you have in common with them that will help deepen the connection they feel to your campaign? What do you both care about?
- Why is your campaign important? By now, you should be able to repeat the reasons in your sleep. If you need help answering this question, take time to reread *Step 2: Make Your Case*.
- How will your donors see results? Briefly explain again the impact of their contributions. Make this statement both confident and direct. For example, "Because of your efforts, 25 children will be able to attend an after-school program designed to improve their grades and keep them entertained in a safe, loving environment."
- How big a contribution are you asking for? What did you ask for during your meeting or phone call? You will ask for the same range or gift level again in your letter. Refer to your notes or Fundraising Pyramid to obtain a specific range for each letter.
- How can they contribute? Don't make it hard for them to send a check. Include easy instructions on how to donate.

Style Matters

If you are not confident in your writing ability, get help from one of your members or stakeholders. If you want to give it a try, keep the following style tips in mind:

- Use "You" and 'I.' You are writing to one person, so speak to that person directly. Avoid labels such as "donors" or "contributors" because that is not how they identify themselves. Write like you are talking to them. For example, "I am asking for your help...."
- Ask more than once. Don't wait until the end of the letter to ask for money. Repeat your request, underscoring the importance of the gift.
- Make it easy on the eye. Format your letters so key sentences and phrases stand out. You can use bold or underlined words throughout the letter to make your point, just don't use

them too often. Try not to include more than five to seven sentences per paragraph.

- End on a positive note. Your letter should have an uplifting ending that again stresses the difference this campaign can make and how their monetary gift will help make it happen.

Common Mistakes To Avoid

Here's a list of things to avoid when writing a letter to your donors:

- Don't use a letter to recruit. The goal is to motivate, not recruit. Do not ask for money if no one from your organization has spoken to the recipient. You obtain stakeholders through personal contact, not cold letters. In order for a letter to be effective, there must be an existing relationship.
- Never ask blindly for large gifts. If you are asking for a large amount of money (what counts as "large" is relative to each organization), make the ask during a face-to-face meeting. It can turn off major donors to receive a big request without personal interaction. Again, never make your donors feel like cash machines.
- Don't bury the ask under too much copy. Get to the point. This is a brief letter, not a book.
- Don't use overly flowery or sentimental language. Too many adjectives or adverbs can make your letter sound pretentious or phony instead of genuinely enthusiastic.
- Avoid long and run-on sentences. Many stakeholders will not read your letter word for word. They will scan it. Short sentences will convey your message more effectively as their eyes move down the page.
- Use proper grammar and spelling. This should go without saying, but you might be surprised by how many letters contain errors. Check, double check, and triple check all of your correspondence. Then, give it to a few other people to proofread before you send.

Examples

As chief executive officer and president of TMCF, I am responsible for sending motivational letters to our stakeholders. Here are a couple that have yielded excellent results.

Dear «Salutation»,

As one of the thousands of recepients who have graduated from public Historically Black Colleges and Universities (HBCUs), it's my greatest pleasure to thank you for your past support of the Thurgood Marshall College Fund (TMCF). Your generosity makes it possible for deserving students to achieve their dream of a college education. It is an investment in more than 215,000 talented young people.

The scholarship award from TMCF made a difference in my life. Prior to receiving the Thurgood Marshall scholarship, I dropped out of school twice for financial reasons. I felt hopeless until I heard about TMCF. Today, TMCF is still making a difference in the lives of many students.

Your support enables TMCF to continue its mission of supporting the education and career development of thousands of scholars every year. In addition to awarding merit scholarships, your gift helped TMCF diversify its programs support to include new initiatives.

Prominent among its new programs is the creation of *The Leadership Institute* in 2000. The Leadership Institute affords students attending the 47-member public HBCUs training in leadership skills. This program, which is run by top corporate executives from diverse fields, is specifically designed to prepare students to assume leadership roles upon graduation.

TMCF is also strongly dedicated to strengthening the technology capacities of its member schools through millions of dollars worth of technology grants it has received during the past year from IBM, Hewlett-Packard and Microsoft Corporation.

With your help, TMCF can do more to continue the legacy of Thurgood Marshall, Sr., by providing access and opportunity for those who, like me, have a dream.

Sincerely,

P.S. Please make your gift to TMCF today, to provide a better tomorrow for several bright young men and women.

Dear Mr./Mrs. Last Name:

On behalf of the more than 1,000 students benefiting from our after school programs, I am pleased to submit a request for a grant of $5,000 to support the continuation of the Sunnyside After school program. The program will be administered by (name of organization).

(History of your organization and few data points)
(sample) The Thurgood Marshall College Fund member schools are a crucial source of higher education for African Americans. While they account for 15 % of African American post-secondary students, they award 35% of the baccalaureate degrees earned by African Americans. Fifty-six percent (56%) of law degrees earned by African Americans are awarded by TMCF schools. Fifty-eight percent (58%) of all African American public schoolteachers graduated from Thurgood Marshall schools. Howard and Morgan State Universities are among the top providers of Doctorates in Insurance Studies for African Americans. Each year, the Fund's member schools provide 1,100 different majors and professional certification programs.

The enclosed proposal will provide you with a detailed overview of the need for the after school program and important role it plays in the community. I hope that you will join our volunteers and parents in supporting this important initiative. I can be reached at (insert phone number), if you should have any additional questions or comments.

Sincerely,

Dwayne Ashley

*"Volunteers are like Family.
They have to be in the trenches with the
organization's mission."*

CHAPTER 6

The Sixth Step: Work the Phones

Telemarketing can be a great way to reach your stakeholders. Still, many fundraisers hate the thought of picking up the phone. We've all been hassled so many times by telemarketers over the years that the very idea of conducting a phone campaign can make us shudder. So why do it? It works! You just need to know how to do it right.

A well-run telephone campaign benefits you by:
- Strengthening relationships with your donors
- Finding out what your donors are interested in, therefore allowing you to tailor your requests to them
- Helping you update your contact information
- Providing you with a cost-effective way to ask for money
- Giving you a chance to say thank-you.

A well-run telephone campaign benefits your donors/stakeholders by:
- Keeping them informed on your current campaign
- Making them feel like they are an important part of your efforts
- Giving them a chance to hear from those they have helped
- Providing an easy way for them to give money.

The Telemarketing Process

Before you start dialing, you need to know exactly what you want to accomplish. Some goals are purely financial. Others focus on getting the word out. Do you want to raise $15,000, receive 100 new pledges of support, or spread the word about your new campaign to every one of your stakeholders? Once you decide on your goals, write them on a big piece of paper and post it where your volunteers can see. Updating it as you make progress will add to the campaign's momentum and increase your callers' enthusiasm. Although phone campaigns can be very cost effective, they are not free. You will need to account for all costs associated with telemarketing and add them onto your fundraising goals.

Common expenses include:
- Renting phones
- Renting a facility if you do not already have one
- Printed materials for volunteers
- Refreshments for volunteers.

The List

I do not recommend relying on cold calling for the same reasons I don't like sending out cold letters. You don't want the first time someone hears about your organization to be over the phone. The vast majority of people you call will immediately become suspicious if they pick up the phone and get a sales pitch from someone they don't know. You are likely to annoy them with this type of telemarketing, which means they will not only ignore your request now, they'll probably ignore you in the future. Instead, call people from your list of stakeholders. You should have developed a comprehensive list already, based on the information in Chapter 1. Your stakeholders will usually welcome a chance to hear from you. If you have reached them at a bad time, they'll be more likely to forgive the interruption.

Your Calling Team

There is no way you are going to be able to make all of these phone calls yourself, so you will have to rely on your board members and volunteers. I always create my pool of volunteers by gathering a group of beneficiaries. If you are raising money for a youth baseball league, get the kids to make the calls. If the children are too young, enlist their parents. If you are supporting services for a health organization, ask some of the recepients to make the calls. At TMCF, we have students make calls to the donors who have helped pay for their scholarships. More than anyone else, your beneficiaries know the value of the service you provide. They are the embodiment of your mission. Beneficiaries provide instant shared affinity with your stakeholders. To illustrate this point, put yourself in the place of your donor. Let's say you have graduated from XYZ University. One day, you receive a telemarketing phone call from the university asking for money for a sports program. As a graduate, are you more likely to get a warm, fuzzy feeling talking to a paid staff member or a student who says he is starting his sophomore year and is really looking forward to this year's football season? Talking to the student instantly reminds you of the autumn days you spent on campus, watching the games with your friends. These warm memories are your shared affinity. It's pretty hard to brush off or hang up on someone you have such a connection with.

Create a Script

Write a script to use as a guideline. Although you want to encourage your callers to speak from the heart and not sound like they are reading, a script will help them if they get stuck. What you write depends on your goals. However, every script should contain some basics.

Make sure your script:
- Immediately identifies the caller and the organization
- Makes the shared affinity known
- Includes one or two sentences on the campaign's mission
- Asks the donor for a specific range of support
- Thanks the donor.

Training Your Callers

Beneficiaries are the best people to make phone calls for you, but they most likely will need more training than your staff, board members, or other stakeholders. It is a good idea to hold a training session the day before your campaign begins.

Gather your callers together and brief them on:
- The mission. Tell them why this campaign is important and how they are going to help.
- The goals. Explain your phone campaign's goals. Show them the poster with the goals outlined.
- The script. Go over the script and ask them if they have any questions. Encourage them memorize the key points, but stress that they don't have to know it word for word. Ask them to study it until they feel they can carry out a phone

call without sounding like they are reading a canned script. It is also a good idea to go through a role-playing scenario where they can hear how a phone call might sound.

- The schedule. Make sure everyone knows what time they should show up and how long they will work.
- The Tools. Go over everything they will have in front of them when making calls.
- The Rules. Explain the ethics of holding a telephone campaign and what to do if they can not answer a donor's question. (I'll have more on this in the next section.) During the meeting, ask your beneficiaries to share their concerns and questions. Try to keep the mood light and fun. Stress that you and other leaders will be around to help them if they have any problems. Most importantly, thank them for their efforts.

Ground Rules

You can avoid angering and alienating your stakeholders by sticking to the following rules:

- Don't call during dinner! Poor timing is the number-one complaint stakeholders have about receiving telephone solicitations. You have a window of opportunity that is only open after dinner until about 9 p.m.
- Keep track of the list! Cross off names as you contact people. Calling the same people more than once will only make them angry.
- Listen! Don't be so eager to collect money that you don't hear what your stakeholders are trying to tell you.
- Never coerce! Never try to force someone to give money. If people say "no," thank them and end the phone call. Keeping someone on the phone who doesn't want to talk to you will only hurt your organization's reputation.
- Be honest! If you can't answer a donor's question, put a leader on the phone or make arrangements for someone to call back with the information. Never guess or make up answers.

- Don't make promises you can't keep! Creating false expectations will permanently lose the trust of your stakeholders.

Assisting Your Volunteers

Despite your volunteers' shared affinity with stakeholders, not everyone they call is going to be pleasant. Typically, volunteers will become less enthusiastic after hearing a few "no's." If they are discouraged, their energy level will drop. More donors will then sense their lack of enthusiasm and respond negatively, which will make volunteers even more tentative about making phone calls. It's a downward spiral. You can help your volunteers avoid becoming burned out by reminding them that hearing "no" is simply a part of fundraising. Tell them it does not mean they are doing a bad job. Stakeholders who say "no" now may change their mind in the future. As long as the telemarketer is politely planting seeds of interest, he or she is doing a good job. It is also important to schedule short shifts and provide frequent breaks and refreshments in order to keep energy levels high. Increase the success of telemarketing by giving your callers the tools they need to do their job.

All volunteers should have:

- The list of numbers they are responsible for
- The written script
- A question-and-answer sheet of common questions they may receive
- A one-page sheet that highlights key information about your organization and its goals. This may come in handy if a donor has a question that is not limited to the campaign.
- Forms to log who they've called and the response they received
- Pen and pad for notes. If a caller has a question they can not answer, they should write down the donor's question and phone number so a member of your staff can call back with the requested information.

"If neighborhood gossip isn't talking about your project….then you are not marketing."

CHAPTER 7

The Seventh Step: Market Your Project

Even the best programs will wither if no one knows about them. We've talked about spreading the word through meetings and phone calls. Now, it is time to tackle marketing. If you are new to marketing, the best advice I can give you is to find a team member or stakeholder who is a marketing professional or member of the media. Bring this person into your campaign and put him or her in charge of marketing. You can't learn successful marketing strategies in one day or from reading one chapter of a book. Seriously, get help from someone who does it for a living.

Your Marketing Plan

You can help your marketing expert by providing the information. He or she needs to understand your goals– whether you are trying to raise money, public awareness, or both. Be realistic when discussing your goals. You need a marketing plan that is achievable, not so far-reaching that you'll never be able to accomplish it. You also have to clearly communicate how much you have to spend. You are not going to get the exposure of a million dollar campaign on a $100 marketing budget.

Your collateral, which is the printed material that explains your organization and campaign, should not be too glitzy. Do not send the message to donors that you are spending their money on expensive marketing. You can avoid this problem by getting someone to donate printing services and/or materials. Then acknowledge the donating by putting, "Printing materials donated by ABC Copy Services," somewhere on the collateral pieces. This is a great way to thank the company that provided the service, while letting your donors know you are responsible with your expenses.

Fundraising Over the Internet

The Internet is rapidly expanding fundraising options. Years ago, some fundraisers recoiled at the idea of online campaigns, saying that their donors would never go for it. Then, as familiarity with the Internet grew, other fundraisers predicted that web fundraising would replace most other campaign methods. I firmly believe that both ideas were wrong. The reality of fundraising is that online marketing is an important tool that should not be ignored. But it can't replace face-to-face fundraising. Remember that people give to people, not to organizations or websites. Online fundraising is most effective when it is used in combination with traditional, face to-face interaction with your donors.

The benefits of online marketing include:

- It is cost effective. Operating a website and sending emails can be a very inexpensive way to reach your donors.
- You can immediately give your supporters updates on your campaign.
- Many donors enjoy the immediacy of the Internet. They can access you 24 hours a day, seven days a week.
- An increasing number of people pay their bills and make donations online. They don't want to write out checks and mail envelopes. Lack of an online option reduces the chances that they will give to you.
- People who don't receive your calls or mailings can still learn about your programs. This works especially well for those who want to support a cause like yours but have never made direct contact with you.
- Some people don't like traditional campaign methods. They don't want a meeting. They don't want a phone call. They simply want to give their annual donation without hearing from you.

Create a Website

I recommend that every fundraising organization have a website. It does not need to be expensive or elaborate. Thanks to new service options, operating a website has become easy and inexpensive. Many web hosting plans will provide design tools and data storage for a very small monthly fee. If you are unsure about how to develop a website, enlist help from one of your team members, volunteers, or stakeholders. You are bound to find someone who is knowledgeable in this area.

Once you have a hosting service, your website should include:
- Your mission
- Your presentation package
- Your case
- A few pictures that help tell your story
- A way for people to give. You can set up programs that allow them to give via credit card. Some organizations simply have an online form where potential donors can input in their names and contact information so a team member can reach them. No matter how you decide to handle this, just make sure there is a way that people can make a gift.

Don't Spam

I am always sensitive to the fact that people receive a lot of unwanted emails. I never want them to associate my organization's name with spam. If you want to send emails, keep them very brief. Emails can be a good way to inform stakeholders and volunteers about new developments. However, I do not recommend that you use them to make an ask. Your emails should be to relay news, not overtly solicit. That said, make sure to include a link to your web page on all emails. That way, email recipients are just a click away from giving if they choose.

Combining Outreach Methods

Online fundraising works best when it is part of a comprehensive fundraising campaign. Don't miss a chance to maximize your efforts by combining outreach methods. I recommend printing your organization's website and email addresses on ALL collateral material and mailings. This small addition to your marketing materials can dramatically boost traffic to your website. A donor who picks up one of your flyers may decide to give later online. A stakeholder who gets a letter might like to check for campaign updates by going to your website.

The goal is to make supporting your programs as convenient as possible for your donors.

When you are faced with a limited amount of money, it can be tempting to focus all of your efforts in one area. If you have reached your goals in the past by holding a phone campaign, you may be reluctant to spend money building an online presence. I understand this. However, don't forget to look at the big picture. Your phone campaign will help you now. Your website will help you all year long. Spending money on a website might not immediately pay off. It will take time to build a presence. You'll have to constantly remind stakeholders that they can now contact you online. Still, the money your website brings in should eventually more than offset its operating costs. Whenever you start a new fundraising campaign, think about ways your website can contribute to the project. Integrate your website into every aspect of your fundraising campaign. You'll find that it will pay off because many of your donors will appreciate the convenience. If you have a website, you can be sure that many other organizations with similar missions and goals also have websites. I encourage you to search for these sites and see what they have to offer. Many provide message boards or online forums that are open to the public. I have gotten some great ideas from these sites and even used them to recruit new volunteers.

Making Marketing Pay Off

Before you can market effectively, you have to know who you should market to. We've talked about creating a list of stakeholders. It is important to update this list frequently. Most organizations lose contact with the majority of their donors over time. You shouldn't have to reinvent your donor base over and over. Keep track of the donors you have and add new ones by making your contact list a priority. If donors give more than one year in a row, they'll be far more likely to become long-term contributors to your organization. The easiest way to track donors is through past giving. Invest the time in building a good computer database that your leadership team can access. Frequently, your donor will even ask you, "How much did I give last year?" You should be prepared to answer the question. Even the best marketing campaign will fail if your donors don't feel as if you care about what they are giving.

CHAPTER 8

The Final Step: Thank and Cultivate Your Donors

Thanking and cultivating your donors is the single most important action you can take to ensure the sustainability of your organization. After all, without the resources of your donors, you wouldn't exist. Your relationships with donors will suffer as soon as they start to feel like it is a "one-way street" where you do all of the taking. People will not continue to give money if they feel they do not get something in return. In the vast majority of cases, what they want is simply to know that you appreciate their contributions and that they are helping you make a difference in the world. You can keep them satisfied by acknowledging them immediately after every gift and making an effort to maintain a relationship with them between donations.

Saying "Thank You"
Thanking your donors:
- Increases the chance of repeat giving
- Increases the chance that the next gift will be at a higher level
- Deepens the connection and loyalty they feel toward your organization.

You can thank your donors in countless ways, but some of the most common approaches to show your appreciation include:
- A handwritten note
- A phone call, followed by a letter or note
- A lunch or dinner to recognize major donors
- A visit to the donor
- An award
- A mention in your group's newsletter.

Keep in mind that although these are all good ways to say thank you, a few of them should be done in conjunction with another expression of thanks. If donors give you a gift, mentioning them in your newsletter is nice, but you had better thank them personally as well. The two most important components of thanking your donor are time and tone. Make it your goal to thank your donor within 24 to 48 hours of receiving a gift. If that is impossible, do it within one week. Your thank-you should feel warm and sincere.

If you are sending a letter, keep in mind that donors don't respond well to impersonal form letters. If you have to send a form letter, at least print one with a personal salutation. Then, try to write a short note at the bottom or personally sign it. No matter how you thank your donors, you should do it in a way that makes them feel good about their gift. Emphasize the positive impact their contributions have on your beneficiaries.

Thank Who?

The short answer is: Thank everyone who helps you in some way. The way you thank them does not have to be elaborate, but each and every gift should be acknowledged. Don't allow any gift to "fall through the cracks." The number-one reason people don't make second gifts is that they got no feedback from their first gift. Some fundraisers say they do not cash a check until after they write the thank-you note. That way, they won't forget to acknowledge their donors because they will be anxious to get the money. That may not always be practical, but it sure will keep you disciplined about sending acknowledgements.

Gift Recognition Policies

The best way to ensure that every donor is properly thanked is to create a gift recognition policy. Make sure members of your leadership team have a copy of the document. Then assign someone to enforce the policy and keep track of all acknowledgements.

How you create your recognition policy depends on the structure of your organization and the average gift amount you receive. Here's a part of a sample gift recognition policy used by a small animal shelter:

- Every donation: A personalized letter, signed by a member of the board
- Donations over $25: A personalized letter and subscription to quarterly newsletter
- Donations over $150: A thank-you card written by a board member and newsletter subscription
- Donations over $250: A phone call from the campaign leader, a follow-up handwritten note, and newsletter subscription
- Donations over $500: Mention of the gift in the bi-annual newsletter, phone call, handwritten note, newsletter subscription, and inclusion in the annual "Paws Together Donor Recognition" reception.

Cultivating Donor Relationships

Cultivating relationships with your donors goes beyond sending thank-you cards. You cultivate by consistently letting your donors know that you appreciate them, not just their checks. There's a tried and true rule in fundraising: If someone gives you $100, they can afford to give $1,000. If they give you $10,000, they can probably give $50,000. However, the first time a donor writes a check to your organization, they are not going to give all they can afford. It's like a courtship. You don't propose marriage on a first date. Getting to know the person you are dating takes time. If you gradually realize that your relationship has the potential to keep you both satisfied over the long term, you consider making a deeper commitment. Donors work the same way. That first check allows them to test the waters and see if you are a serious suitor, worthy of their attention. As your relationship grows, so will their range of giving.

You cultivate donors, which increases their gift levels, by:
- Asking for advice and ideas. My donors come from all walks of life and are savvy in many different areas. As the leader of TMCF, I know that one of our best resources is the knowledge base of our stakeholders. When I have to make a decision, I do not hesitate to seek their input. For example, I might call a donor and say, "I know you are an expert in marketing. We want to spread the message about an exciting new program we are developing. Can I bounce a few ideas

off of you?" The key here is that when I ask for advice, it is because I truly want it. I don't ask trivial questions in a phony attempt to make a donor feel important. Neither should you.

- Sending material. When you complete a research report, send it to stakeholders with a note explaining that you want to keep them updated. If your organization is featured in the local newspaper, send out copies so donors can share the excitement of receiving publicity.
- Remembering details. When I go to see major stakeholders, I ask them about their families, hobbies, or new business ventures. I remember what they tell me. The next time I see them I can say, "Have you been out on your boat this year yet?" or, "I saw your wife's new store on Main Street. It looks great!" They are impressed that I care enough to talk about what matters to them.
- Knowing when to back off. Not every donor wants to be your best friend. If you have stakeholders who are all business, keep your interactions brief and limited to discussions about your campaign.

They'll respect your focused professionalism. Cultivating your donors comes down to knowing them on a personal level. You need to understand their personalities to figure out how to keep them connected to your organization. Every time you thank them, you have an opportunity to cultivate your relationship. Remember, what works for one donor will not work for all.

Thank your donors the way they want to be thanked.
For instance, how do you thank someone you don't talk to but who gives to your organization like clockwork? First, you have to realize that not all donors want public recognition or a profuse display of thanks. TMCF has a major donor who gives a lot of money on a consistent basis. We don't have personal contact with her because she likes to give through her investments.

Several years ago, I found out that this donor likes to know how scholarship recipients have been affected by our program. Now I regularly send her a list of student names and how much they received. This way, she knows exactly who she is supporting. Some donors might not consider this enough of a thank-you, but the list is what she likes, so we make sure she receives it.

Your Donor List

It is important to keep a donor list that includes important information about your donors, including what they have given. Keep track of every donation they make. You will use this list to thank your donors for individual gifts and to cultivate future giving.

Your list should include:
- Donor's name
- Address
- Phone number(s) and fax
- Email address
- Spouse and children's names
- Birthdates of donor and immediate family members
- Relationship history. Include how many times you have visited and called them
- Donations. Keep track of every gift, noting the date, amount, campaign, and method used to solicit the gift. For example: 11/05/05, $500, Leadership Summit, telephone call
- Extra information that might be helpful, such as the donor's interests, hobbies, or memberships in other organizations Most people turn their list into a computer database. However, if you do not have a computer you can keep track your donors by using index cards. Write the name and contact information of each donor on the front and the important information about them on the back. No matter how you store your list, use it as a tool to help establish a rapport with your donors. It's just one more way to make your transactions more meaningful for both parties.

Thank and Cultivate Your Donors
The Checklist

The Thank-you Letter
- Send within 24 to 48 hours after receiving gift.
- Make it warm and sincere.
- Make it personal. Even form letters should have a personal salutation and/or written signature.

Gift Recognition Policies
- Create a policy for every level of giving.
- Distribute the policy to every board member.
- Make one person in charge of enforcing the policy.

Cultivate Your Donors
- Get to know them on a personal level. Remember details about their family, business and hobbies.
- Ask them for advice.
- Keep them updated on your organization's mission and campaign progress.
- Know when to back off. Don't force a relationship.

Your Donor List
- Assign one person to oversee and manage the list.
- Compile information listed on pg. 76.
- Create a computer database or file of index cards.
- Make the list accessible to all board members so they can update it every time they make contact with a donor.
- Assign one person to oversee and manage the list to keep information up-to-date.

CHAPTER 9

Planning an Event

When you mention a "special event" fundraiser, many people automatically think of black-tie cocktail parties and fancy, catered dinners. While these examples certainly qualify as event fundraisers, there are many other types of projects that fall into the same category. Event fundraisers are simply planned occasions that bring together your supporters at a certain time and place.

Some of the most common event fundraisers include:
- Auctions
- Athletic events, such as a walk or 5K run
- Car washes
- Bake sales
- Raffles
- Meal-based events, like pancake breakfasts or spaghetti feasts
- Carnivals
- Book fairs (these are a favorite source of income for schools and PTAs)

Event Pros and Cons
Events are a good way to:
- Raise awareness. You can often reach people that you might not otherwise have contact with. For example, drivers who have never heard of you might stop at your car wash just because they see your volunteers holding signs on the side of the road. If you do a good job, they'll leave with not only a clean vehicle but also a positive impression of your organization. You might even end up with some new donors and volunteers.

- Mobilize your base. Events are a good way to further motivate the people who already support you.
- Raise money. Unlike long campaigns, certain types of events give you a chance to raise a lot of money in a short period of time. A successful auction relying on donated items and refreshments can bring in a significant amount of money in just a few hours.
- Reward donors. A well-planned event can be a nice way to celebrate the people who make your programs possible.

For instance, your annual chili cook-off might be something your major donors look forward to attending every year. This type of event gives your donors a chance to congregate, reinforcing the positive feeling of belonging to your organization. Despite the benefits of throwing an event, this type of fundraising has plenty of drawbacks. Consider the following before you get carried away with the excitement of planning:

- Time and effort. Events usually take more time and effort to plan than other types of fundraising. Throwing an event is hard work!
- Cost. Events require you to spend money before you can make it. You may have to pay for a facility, food, decorations, logistics, and many other necessities long before the event.
- The gamble. Many event fundraisers fail to bring in the amount of money projected. There are a number of reasons this can happen, including bad planning, marketing, and weather. Before you throw an event, ask yourself if you can really afford to have it fail.

Choosing Your Event

Reflect Your Mission

If you are going to hold an event, you need to make sure that you select one that fits your organization's goals and overall mission. Not all events work equally well for everyone. For instance, if you are raising money for playground equipment in your local park, throwing a black-tie wine tasting will seem out of sync with your mission. It will not match the values behind your project.

A family event offering entertainment for children will be more appropriate. Likewise, if you are raising money for an association that assists entrepreneurs, you shouldn't hold an event for children. Instead, you should pick a more upscale, professional venue that reflects the goals of your beneficiaries.

The size of your event also matters. Large groups will have to hold larger events in order to reach their broad base of donors and beneficiaries. Small groups will have an easier time funding and managing an event requiring fewer volunteers and donors to make it successful.

When and Where

You will have to rule out some events simply because of timing. First, ask yourself when you need to start reaping the benefits of the event. If you are raising money to help victims of a recent hurricane, you need to pull together something quickly. Therefore, you can't book a venue for a date 10 months from now. Even if you have some flexibility with timing, there are still important issues to consider:

- What else is going on? Pick a time and place that does not compete with other planned activities, especially if the other scheduled events are popular. In other words, don't hold your small carnival at the same time as the big county fair.
- Location, location, location. If you want to get people to attend your event, hold it close by. Most people don't want to travel a long distance. Also avoid areas known for heavy traffic or anything else that might make getting to your event a hassle.
- Volunteer availability. Know about situations that might make it tough for your volunteers to help you. If you rely on college students, don't throw an event when they are taking finals.

Your Event Budget

Creating a budget for an event can be tricky because there are so many variables, and you will encounter unexpected expenses. You may have money to rent a hall, but what about the required security deposit? What will it cost to clean up after your event? Do you need to buy supplies like trash bags, or can someone donate them? Costs are always higher the first three years you hold an event. In Chapter 1, I told you that your campaign costs should comprise 10 to 40 percent of your total budget. This estimate does not apply to new events.

When throwing an event for the first time, be prepared to spend up to 80 percent of your proceeds on event costs. I know, it's shocking! However, as you grow, your costs will go down and your profits will go up. Each year, you will become better at running the event. You'll hopefully gain more sponsors, broaden your revenue base, and learn from any initial mistakes you make. By the third year of throwing an annual event, your campaign costs should fall more into an acceptable range of around 33 percent. So why hold an event if you aren't going to make much money?

Remember, not all benefits are financial. New events can raise awareness of your organization and give you a platform for thanking your donors, However if after the first three years, your costs are way above 33 percent, it is time to consider discontinuing the event unless you are reaping major rewards in other ways.

Reducing Costs

- You can probably come up with a creative idea to reduce costs for every item on your budget. Here are some things to consider:
- Space. Local restaurants might be willing to let you use their party room as a way to get more people through the door. You'll be most likely to get a donated venue during off-peak or slow times. It will be much harder to find a donated space during the busy holiday season or on Saturday nights.
- Food. If you are holding a chicken barbeque, ask a local grocery store to sign on as a sponsor and donate some or all of the food. Also ask restaurants and caterers for food donations. In return, keep a stack of their business cards and/or menus where guests can pick them up.
- Entertainment. Deejays who are trying to build their business may be willing to provide entertainment to increase their name recognition within the community.

- Printing. Any local business or organization can help you pay for printing costs. Just make sure to thank them for their contribution somewhere on the printed material.

Your Event Timeline

Timelines vary dramatically from event to event. Some groups have successfully thrown events in several weeks, while others start planning their annual events a year in advance. The only thing that really matters when devising a timeline is that you leave enough time to take care of all of the details. List everything you need to accomplish before the event. Then, arrange each item according to how much advance time it requires. It can be a good idea to create a weekly checklist leading up to the event.

Below is an example of an eight-week timeline for a silent auction to be held at a local country club. This is a basic outline and would require the addition of specific details, such as picking a menu and creating a volunteer work schedule.

Week 1
- Hold first planning meeting with leadership team.
- Create a list of prospective donors and sponsors.

Week 2
- Meet to finalize planning and logistics.
- Make arrangements for printing invitations and fundraising letter.
- Finish stakeholder list and begin contacting potential donors and sponsors.

Week 3
- Meet with venue staff, caterers, and entertainers.
- Determine speakers and flow of activity for evening.
- Finalize list of items to be auctioned.
- Give each committee member the final plans for the event.

Week 4
- Mail letters and invitations.

Week 5
- Meet with donors.
- Complete all arrangements with caterers, entertainers, speakers and venue.

Week 6
- Make follow-up calls to donors.

Week 7 (Event)
- Review plans for event.
- Prepare name tags.
- Create a last-minute checklist.
- Give final count of guests to caterer.

Week 8 (Follow-up)
- Make sure you've received all money from auctioned items.
- Send thank-you letters.
- Review event to see if it met goals, including financial, attendance, and awareness.
- Make leadership team aware of final outcome and any issues that need to be addressed.

Determining Your Success

There are many different ways to determine if your event was successful. It all depends on what you hoped to achieve. For example, you can measure your success by asking:

- Did you meet your attendance goal?
- Did you receive the revenue you hoped for?
- Were you able to raise a significant amount of public awareness?

For example, each year TMCF holds an event in Washington, D.C., to help people better understand our mission. We consider the event a success, even though it only brings in enough money to pay for itself. Although we don't make a profit, the event succeeds because it gives us a way to interact with the people on Capitol Hill who have a big influence on our nation's educational system.

Events can be a great way to meet your campaign goals. However, don't always assume throwing one is your best option. Neophyte fundraisers tend to get excited about the idea of holding a special event, but their visions of a glamorous evening or fun social gathering often are not based on realistic expectations. Remember, events can require a lot of work for very little financial payoff. Make sure you are clear about what your campaign needs to accomplish before you rush ahead with planning an event.

Planning an Event
The Checklist
Choosing Your Event
- Does the type of event reflect your mission?
- How soon do you need to complete the event?
- What other similar events are being held in the community?
- Will the event location hamper attendance?
- Have you picked a time when your volunteers are available?

Your Event Budget
- List all of your expenses.
- Plan for unexpected expenses.
- Do the math: What percentage of your revenue will go toward event expenses?
- Review your budget in an effort to cut costs.

Create a Timeline
- List all necessary activities prior to event.
- Order activities according to how much preparation time they will require.
- Make a weekly checklist by filling in the "to do" items from your list.
- Fill in additional items as necessary.
- Once it's created, keep a sharp eye on your timeline.

Determining Success
- Consider what you have achieved.
- Did your achievements match your initial goals?
- What unexpected benefits arose from your event?
- What, if anything, went wrong with your event?
- Pass on your findings to your leadership team.
- Discuss ways to make you next event even better.

"Burning issues get new energy and concepts flowing."

CHAPTER 10

Campaign Burning Issues

Just when you think you've got this fundraising business under control, something almost always pops up. I call these "Campaign Burning Issues" because they can burn your campaign to the ground if you're not careful. Campaign burning issues are problems that arise through no fault of your own. They can plague even the best planned projects. You can't always predict what burning issue you'll face, but you always have to be ready to take action. You can't sit around waiting for someone else to put out the fires.

Over the years, I've had to deal with my share of campaign burning issues. Although each situation is unique, problems generally fall into three categories:
- Personnel issues, which can include both your volunteers and leadership team
- Catastrophic events, such as a natural disaster
- Economic downturns that affect the climate of giving.

I'm going explain some common dilemmas in each category and share solutions that have proven successful for me.

Personnel Issues

Promises, Promises
You start a campaign with what appears to be a motivated leadership team. They all confidentially vow to do their share of the work. Things go well for the first few weeks, and then suddenly a few members of your team become harder to reach on the phone, they don't return messages, and when you do reach them, they are vague about the progress they've

made so far. They talked a good game and you believed they would produce results. Instead, you now have a team that is not holding up its end of the bargain.

I've seen this situation time and time again. Part of the problem is the way many boards are formed. Often, non-profits pick people with high public profiles to sit on the board because their names bring attention to the organization. This can be a great idea, unless the members take the term "sitting" on the board too literally. They need to understand from the outset that they are going to have to do more than just sit if they want to take part in the campaign. You need them to perform real legwork.

You can prevent this problem to a certain degree by meeting with each person individually before the start of the campaign. I recently met with a well-known man who expressed interest in being on our board. Although I did not doubt his good intentions, I said to him, "I want you to be part of this board. However, I have to be candid with you. You are going to be expected to raise some money. This will take much more work than just showing up at a few quarterly meetings." He agreed and so far we've had a great working relationship.

When talking to a potential board member about the position:
- Be honest. even if it means losing people you think would bring publicity to your cause. Don't tell them you would be happy just to have them join the organization and sit on the board if you really need them bring in money.
- Let them talk. Ask them about their expectations for the position. If their goals are much different than yours, they might not be the best candidate.
- Get a verbal agreement. Make sure you are on the same page by receiving a verbal pledge. Ask for their promise in a way that sounds respectful, not as if you are lecturing or patronizing them. You can say something as simple as, "So, am I correct in understanding that you are making a commitment to come to our board meetings, help train our phone bank volunteers on November 7th, and use your contacts to bring in an additional $15,000?" Now you

have spelled out exactly what you require. When they say "yes." you have a verbal agreement. Sometimes even having a verbal agreement will not keep board members active in the campaign. I have had to chase them down in the past and say, "I know you are busy, but we need you to fulfill the commitment you made when you agreed to join the board. We can not be successful without your efforts."

You will often face these same issues with volunteers. However, unlike board members, you probably already know that you will lose some volunteers along the way. Plus, volunteers are often easier to replace. Still, always ask your volunteers for a verbal commitment, and don't be afraid to remind them of their promises if necessary.

Death of a Stakeholder

A few times I have had to deal with the death of a major volunteer or donor. On these somber occasions, I have tried to figure out how to honor the wishes of the deceased by still involving them posthumously in the campaign. A way to do this is to ask people to give a gift in honor of this individual's longtime support.

Your volunteer or donor wanted your campaign to succeed, so recognizing them while going forward with the project is usually the best way to handle the situation.

Catastrophic Events

Occasionally something terrible will happen that affects many people on a broad scale. In this case, it can be difficult to determine what course of action to take. You will have to decide if you should postpone your campaign, cancel it completely, or push forward. If you continue, you'll need to consider changing some or all aspects of the campaign in order to appropriately acknowledge the recent events.

TMCF has faced several catastrophic events over the years, but none as devastating as the terrorist attacks on September 11, 2001. TMCF's offices are in New York, so we had to be sensitive not only to our beneficiaries and donors, but also to the staff members who were dealing with personal tragedies. Immediately after the attacks, we took a hard look at our campaigns and programs. Our annual "Leadership Institute Recruitment Conference" was set to be held in New York City just a few weeks later. Each year, the event draws hundreds of top students from *public* Historically Black Colleges and Universities to attend leadership and career management training. We knew that many parents would not be comfortable sending their children to New York so soon after the attacks, so we cancelled it. Although many students look forward to the Institute each year, we knew we were making the right decision. Then we turned our attention to our next big event, which was our 14th Anniversary Awards Dinner, scheduled for December 21 at the Sheraton New York Hotel & Towers. We considered also canceling the dinner. Instead, we decided to go on, but not entirely as originally planned. Although the awards dinner is always a joyful event, we knew we had to recognize the tragedy and honor its victims.

Our dinner was the first major fundraising event to be held in the city after the attacks. Despite our initial trepidation, the event raised a record amount of $1.4 million and was attended by more than 1,600 people, including business leaders and celebrities. Our decision to hold the dinner during a very difficult time in our nation's history proved to be the right one.

The success of the event served as a much-needed inspiration to our supporters, students, our member schools and all others who attended. It also gave us a vehicle to raise more money for merit-based scholarships for students and support for our organization's 47 member schools. By acknowledging the tragedy at the dinner, we were able to exceed our financial goals, maintain our integrity, and continue to be a responsible member of our community.

In the fall of 2005, we were in the middle of a campaign that involved holding breakfasts for our supporters. After Hurricane Katrina, we knew that many of our southern schools were dealing with an enormous crisis. It seemed inappropriate to hold the breakfasts, so we put the project on hold, with plans to resume in December.

As you can see from my examples, there is no single right or wrong way to run a campaign during or soon after a catastrophic event. Often, you will have to rely on gut instinct. No matter what decisions you make, just make sure you act with sensitivity. Your goals should never be only about raising money. To truly serve, you need to respect the needs of your members, donors, beneficiaries, and community – especially during a time of crisis.

Economic Downturns

Unfortunately, economic downturns are part of doing business over a long period of time. When the economy starts to take a nosedive, you can't hide from reality. You may have to lower your campaign goals. If you have sold tickets to an annual event each year for $25, maybe this year you'll have to cut the price to $15. You should also be prepared to lose major donors.

Let's say that you are counting on a local company to give you a sizeable gift again this year. One day, you pick up the newspaper and read that the same company is laying off a large portion of its workforce right before Christmas. Do you go ahead with your meeting scheduled for December 15 with the company's president? If you still go, will you ask for the same large gift they gave last year? You have to be realistic. No matter how worthy your program is, the company is not going to want the publicity that would be generated by giving you money right now. How would they be able to justify funding your program at the same time they are cutting jobs?

In this case, the best course of action is to pick up the phone and call the company president. If you have established a good relationship with your donor, you will be able to be frank with him or her. Say that you've seen the article in the newspaper and you are sorry to hear about the company's difficult times. Let the president know that you will understand if the meeting needs to be cancelled or rescheduled. Leave the next step up to the president. He or she will appreciate and remember your sensitivity, which may lead to even larger donations once the company's financial situation gets under control.

When dealing with any burning issue, you must learn to be very direct. Putting out fires requires action, not roundabout requests and hand-wringing. You must rely on timing and research, especially when navigating catastrophic events or a difficult economy. Weigh the circumstances facing your prospects, stakeholders, and beneficiaries so you know when to make an ask and when to back off.

CHAPTER 11

Ethical Issues

Your reputation is your single most important asset. Without a good reputation, you will never be able to raise money for your organization. Donors only give money to people who they trust and respect. Therefore, whenever you conduct business with vendors, sponsors, and donors you must always act in a way that preserves your good name.

You may be thinking that ethical issues are not your main concern. After all, most fundraisers mean well and they don't set out to deceive the people who support them. However, situations sometimes sneak up on you. Perhaps a potential donor offers to give a large financial gift, but only if you tailor your program to suit his interests. His ideas don't really match your mission, but you really want the big check he is offering. What should you do? Maybe during a presentation, you feel tempted to stretch the truth about your campaign's progress in order to impress your audience. After all, you feel sure you are going to be able to reach your goals eventually, so does it matter if you inflate the numbers just a little bit right now? Figuring out how you feel about these issues now will prevent uncertainty later.

The ethical dilemmas you face as a team leader or board member are often different than those faced by the volunteers who work for you. In this chapter, we are going to first look at some of the big picture situations that may threaten the integrity of your organization. Then, we'll address the issues every member of your team must consider. Finally, I am going to provide a checklist of what your donors should be able to expect from you.

Maintaining Your Organization's Integrity

Integrity begins with you. One mistake in judgment can shake the public's confidence in your organization. If that happens, at best, you face a long, difficult process of rebuilding trust. At worst, your organization will never recover. Three common ethical issues involve handling money, staying true to your word, and knowing when to walk away from a donor.

Financial Integrity

You must be honest about how you handle the money you receive from donors and how you manage expenses and compensation. Be upfront with your stakeholders about what and why you are spending. Always be prepared to show them your budget and an accurate accounting of expenses. New fundraisers rarely have paid staff. However, if your organization grows, you will eventually have to face issues of compensation.

There are many resources available to give you legal advice. I am not going to delve into such complicated matters in this chapter. However, I do want to stress that people should never be paid a percentage of the gifts they bring to your organization. You can provide incentives to fundraisers, such as prizes for the person who sells the most tickets. Just make sure you understand the difference between an incentive and a finder's fee. For more information on the ethics of compensation, I suggest you check out material from the Association of Fundraising Professionals. The website is http://www.afpnet.org.

Your Word

Never promise what you can't deliver. If you say that you are going to send 100 kids to camp this summer, you better be prepared to do it. Then, when the summer is over, you better be able to prove that 100 kids actually attended. I have seen many fundraisers overstate their missions when making their case to donors. They think that if they can make their goals seem grander, they'll be able to bring in more money. They believe such deceptions are just little fibs told to benefit the greater good. Not true. They are lies. It is unethical. And it almost always catches up with them.

Don't be tempted to hide bad news. You are not always going to succeed. Over the years, I have been involved in struggling campaigns. Instead of trying to sugarcoat the situation, I have said to my stakeholders, "We're not doing as well as we hoped. Right now, it does not look like we are going to meet our goals." Instead of being angry or disappointed, my stakeholders have respected my honesty. Donors forgive occasional campaign failure. They never forgive dishonesty. So, if your event runs over budget, tell the truth. Your donors, board members, and key volunteers will work with you to correct the situation if you have a good relationship with them. Don't be afraid to talk to them as if they are your family. In this case, you are a family of people working toward common goals. You're on the same team.

Donor's Influence

Donor influence can be an insidious problem. You start out trying to cultivate a good relationship by involving your stakeholders and instead end up relinquishing too much control over your campaign. This sticky situation can lead to unethical behavior and keep you from accomplishing your goals.

Let's say your organization provides an after-school program for at-risk youth. You want to build on the program by offering more math tutors. A prospective donor says he is willing to write a huge check that will pay for all of the tutors. It's a bigger gift than you even hoped he would give. The catch is that he is very concerned about sex education in schools. He also wants to provide mentors to teach your young beneficiaries about abstinence. Now you have a problem. Even if you think that teaching abstinence is a good idea, is it really a good idea for your program? Weren't you and your stakeholders focused on improving mathematical test scores? There are many reasons to be concerned, including:

- First, you don't want the controversy that is sure to arise from his plan. After all, not all of your stakeholders share his values.
- Second, you have limited time with the students each day. You feel they need all that time to study.
- Most importantly, you don't want an outside party to dictate how you serve your beneficiaries. His plan changes your mission!

If you want to preserve the integrity of your program, you must decline the donor's gift, even if it means you will not be able to pay for all of the math tutors you originally wanted. Thank him for his offer but explain that you are not the best charity to receive his gift. If possible, direct him to another organization that shares his vision. Now, let's say that same donor wants to pay for your math tutors, but would also like to start an English as a Second Language (ESL) program. He offers to pay for an additional tutor to help non-native speakers. You hadn't considered this option, but it makes sense. You've noticed that several of your newly immigrated students are having trouble communicating. Perhaps while most of your beneficiaries study math, a few students could work on their language skills. This program could work because it doesn't change your mission, it expands it in a way that offers more programs for your beneficiaries. Donors will often have ideas that can improve your level of service. Don't be so rigid that you refuse to consider them.

However, never change your primary mission just to increase the amount of money you receive. Understand the difference between true philanthropy and requests that are self-serving.

Your Code of Conduct

As a team leader, you have to be clear about how you will conduct yourself and what behavior you expect from everyone who works on your campaign. You cannot predict every awkward or unexpected situation that might pop up. Still, you can reduce the chance of making a reputation-ruining error by creating an Ethical Code of Conduct before you begin any fundraising project.

The details contained in a organization's code of conduct can vary, depending on the type of service provided. Universal items in your policy should include:

- No coercion. Fundraising volunteers should never use coercive tactics to obtain a gift. Donors should never feel like they were forced into giving.
- Behavior. Volunteers should maintain professional decorum at all times. Spell out what this means for your organization, such as "no consumption of alcohol while at an event."
- Decision making. Be very specific about which decisions must be made by a leader or board member.

When creating your code of conduct, do not leave room for ambiguity. Be as specific as possible in order to prevent damaging mistakes.

Donors' Rights

It can be easy to focus so much on your mission that you forget that your donors also have rights. In fact, there is even a document called "The Donor Bill of Rights" that was created by the American Association of Fund Raising Counsel (AAFRC), Association for Healthcare Philanthropy (AHP), the Association of Fundraising Professionals (AFP), and the Council for Advancement and Support of Education (CASE). It is a good idea to share this Bill of Rights with all members of your fundraising team. Include it in the packet of material they receive when they begin to work on your campaign.

The Donor Bill of Rights

Philanthropy is based on voluntary action for the common good. It is a tradition of giving and sharing that is primary to the quality of life. To ensure that philanthropy merits the respect and trust of the general public, and that donors and prospective donors can have full confidence in the nonprofit organizations and causes they are asked to support, we declare that all donors have these rights:

1. To be informed of the organization's mission, of the way the organization intends to use donated resources, and of its capacity to use donations effectively for their intended purposes.
2. To be informed of the identity of those serving on the organization's governing board, and to expect the board to exercise prudent judgment in its stewardship responsibilities.
3. To have access to the organization's most recent financial statements.
4. To be assured their gifts will be used for the purposes for which they were given.
5. To receive appropriate acknowledgement and recognition.
6. To be assured that information about their donation is handled with respect and with confidentiality to the extent provided by law.
7. To expect that all relationships with individuals representing organizations of interest to the donor will be professional in nature.

8. To be informed whether those seeking donations are volunteers, employees of the organization or hired solicitors.
9. To have the opportunity for their names to be deleted from mailing lists that an organization may intend to share.
10. To feel free to ask questions when making a donation and to receive prompt, truthful and forthright answers.

CONCLUSION

When I started out as a fundraiser, I was a complete neophyte. I had no idea how to go about achieving my goals. Although I learned quickly, my road to success would have been much faster and smoother if I had been given a list of easy-to-follow steps. That's why I've created this book for you. I want to avoid seeing other new fundraisers struggle unnecessarily. Your vision for your programs should never have to be clouded by confusion over how to raise money.

I hope this book gave you some insight on how to really make your program a success. You should now know the basics of how to raise money, recruit volunteers, and build an infrastructure that will give your organization sustainability. Even after you've read this book, keep it close by for future reference.

The checklists at the end of many chapters can help you when you need a quick frame of reference for a fundraising activity. Now your real work begins! I wish you much success as you venture forward, making a positive impact and helping our world become a better place.

"Success in Philanthropy is built on the depth of your relationships."

ABOUT THE AUTHOR

Dwayne Ashley, the Chief Executive Officer and President of the Thurgood Marshall College Fund (TMCF) is a 19 year non-profit and fundraising executive. As CEO, he guides TMCF to achieve its mission, as a comprehensive higher education assistance organization representing 47 *public* Historically Black Colleges and Universities. Mr. Ashley leads the organization's long-term planning and guides the overall strategic direction of the organization.

Under his leadership, TMCF surpassed $68 million in support raised for scholarships, capacity building and programs, which represents an increase of more than 1400 percent, and 85 percent of the organization's gross revenues since its founding in 1987.

Mr. Ashley joined Thurgood Marshall College Fund in 1999 as Executive Director, and was appointed president the following year.

Career Path
Mr. Ashley is a 19 year fundraising and non profit veteran with more than $100 million being raised throughout his career. He began fundraising as a college student for the United Negro College Fund. Throughout his career, he has worked for United Way of the Texas Gulf Coast, UNCF, 100 Black Men of America. In his sophomore year of college, he served as an LBJ Intern at the Federal Judicial Center in Washington, where he first met the late Associate Justice Thurgood Marshall.

Education
He graduated Cum Laude with a Bachelor of Science from Wiley College, Texas' oldest historically black college; He earned his master's degree in Governmental Administration from the University of Pennsylvania's Fel's School of Government. He has continued to sharpen his skills

with continuing education and earned Executive Certifications from the Indiana School of Philanthropy's Fundraising Program, and the Texaco Non Profit Executive Leadership Program.

Dwayne Ashley is a native of Houston, Texas with strong roots to his family in Louisiana. He currently resides in New Jersey. He is a writer and is currently working on several books on non profit management, fundraising, and youth career development.